KARIN REHBEIN

LOUISE NATHHORST

ERIC LETTE

NUNO PALMA

KLAUS KRZISCH

KLAUS BALKENHOL

LUIS DOMECQ

CARL HESTER

PIERRE DE BASTARD

SVEN ROTHENBERGER

MARGIT OTTO-CRÉPIN

ANDREAS HAUSBERGER

J FILIPE GIRALDES FIGUEIREDO

CHRISTINE STÜCKELBERGER

KYRA KYRKLUND

MARTIN SCHAUDT

TINEKE BARTELS

STEPHEN CLARKE

ANTONIO DOMECQ

LARA GREENWAY

MONICA THEODORESCU

NICOLE UPHOFF-BECKER

NEIL DOUEK

WOLFGANG EDER

VISIONS
— OF —
DRESSAGE

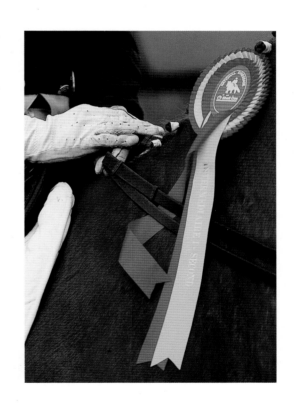

VISIONS

— OF —

DRESSAGE

ELIZABETH
FURTH

THE LYONS PRESS

Dedication

To Annie – a wonderful woman.

British Library Cataloguing-in-Publication Data.
A catalogue record for this book is available from the British Library.

ISBN 0 85131 730 8

Published in Great Britain in 1998 by
J. A. Allen & Company Limited,
1 Lower Grosvenor Place, Buckingham Palace Road,
London, SW1W OEL.

Designed by Design/Section, Frome, England.
Colour Separation by Tenon & Polert Colour Scanning Co. Ltd., Hong Kong.
Printed by Dah Hua International Printing Press Co. Ltd., Hong Kong.

Frontispiece: Anky van Grunsven and Bonfire during their freestyle at the 1996 Atlanta Olympics where the pair won an individual and a team silver medal.

Acknowledgements

My thanks go to Kodak for their generous support in providing me with numerous rolls of excellent film throughout the production of this book.

My warmest thanks also go to my processing lab, Sky Photographic Services, for their compassion and support. I have used them for fourteen years and their generous offer to develop a great number of films for this book free of charge was an enormous help. In particular, I would like to thank Tracy Judge for her good humour, efficiency and encouragement.

I am also very grateful to the Anglo Austrian Society for financing my flight to Vienna to photograph the Spanish Riding School and for getting me back to London in one piece on Austrian Airlines.

It was thanks to TAP – Air Portugal, and Emilia Saunders's generous offer to fly me to Lisbon and back that I was able to capture the beautiful Lusitano horses in action.

A big thank you also goes to Sherene Rahmatallah, honorary member of the Lusitano Breed Society of Great Britain, for her invaluable help in collecting many of the signatures of the Portuguese riders.

I am very grateful to Luz Marlene Rodriquez for her help in communicating with the Domecq family on my behalf.

My appreciation goes to all the riders and the two judges for without their willing participation in sharing their views and impressions this book would never have been as colourful as it is.

Finally, the most precious contributors have been the horses themselves – the true stars of dressage.

CONTENTS

PREFACE

Putting together *Visions of Dressage* has allowed me to take a closer look at the sport of dressage as well as exploring its origins. Dressage as we see it today, performed by competitors around the world, owes its development to the classical training methods of our ancestors. It is for this reason that I have dedicated the first chapter to those institutions whose *raison d'être* it is to keep alive the traditions of classical riding. Talking to competitors and judges, I found out that although the dressage fraternity seems at times to be divided between purists who endorse the classical training methods and those who have developed their own systems, top horsemen and women all respect the importance of the roots of dressage.

Further, it was interesting to discover that only a few enthusiasts believe that dressage could actually be classified as an art form. None the less, I still hold the rather romantic view that training a horse to the highest level of its potential must be close to art as it is obvious for all to see that horse and rider are creating something quite magnificent! Some riders associated the word 'art' too closely with something artificial and were quick to argue that dressage is by no means artificial because the horse's natural movements are always honoured.

It was fascinating to hear how all top-class riders talked about the importance of 'growing' with their horses. They all pointed out that the partnership they share with their animals is based on hours spent in trying to understand them. The dedication that such riders put into earning their horses' trust and achieving the harmony they are striving for deserves tremendous admiration. Interviewing them has reinforced my view that a successful human relationship works along the same principles. However, the key factor is that in neither case does such closeness happen overnight!

Talking to British dressage judge Stephen Clarke and to Eric Lette, Chairman of the FEI (Fédération Equestre Internationale) Dressage Committee, has thrown some light on the complexity of their jobs. At the same time, it was most refreshing to sense the passion for dressage that these two men openly revealed. Strangely enough, none of the riders could actually tell me what it was that attracted them to dressage other than the fascination of obtaining harmony between them and their equine partners.

Photographing dressage at competitions is trickier than photographing any of the other equestrian disciplines because dressage horses are highly sensitive to the slightest disturbance. Occasionally, the click of a camera, or rather ten cameras at the same time, can provoke certain horses to lose their concentration. When riding Rembrandt, Nicole Uphoff-Becker used to be especially nervous about photographers because her partner was very easily put off by the noise of a few shutters going off simultaneously. Photographers are therefore generally placed relatively far away from the arena, which means that we have to work with very long lenses in order to capture stimulating pictures.

Creating *Visions of Dressage* has helped me to learn more about the dressage world. I hope that you will enjoy the collection of images as well as the countless contributions the riders have made. By sharing anecdotes and revealing their emotions, they have generously allowed us into their universe.

FOREWORD

Belgian judge Mariette Withages-Dieltjens

It is with great pleasure that I write the foreword to Elizabeth Furth's *Visions of Dressage*.

Dressage is a unique sport and there are several ways to look at it and picture it. With her camera and her pen, Elizabeth is able to capture people's souls as well as the essence of a moment or situation. The result is amazing!

This superb book is an invitation to enjoy our discipline even more. I hope that everyone will enjoy this piece of art as much as I do.

With my most sincere congratulations to the author.

M. Withages

CLASSICAL DRESSAGE

Preparing this chapter on classical dressage gave me the opportunity to travel to Austria, Portugal, Spain and France, all countries where the traditions of the classical training methods are kept alive.

My first stop was Vienna and the majestic building of the Hofburg, home to the Spanish Riding School and the famous white Lipizzaner stallions. There, I was allowed to watch and photograph the morning training sessions of the riders, chief riders and apprentices of the school. Although the setting of the Winterschule, the indoor school, which, until 1894, was still used for balls and concerts, is exquisite to say the least, it caused a few technical problems in that there was insufficient light to capture the horses in movement. However, thanks to ever-improving film, I was able to get good results by using the Kodak multi-speed negative film rated at 2000 ASA.

At this point I would also like to point out that none of the pictures taken during the morning sessions were posed. There are usually as many as ten horses, if not more, in the arena at a time and one has to be very lucky to frame a horse performing an interesting movement without suddenly having another rider coming into shot!

Not all the pictures in the following pages were taken in Vienna. Between 10.00 am and noon, when the paying public are allowed to watch the schooling sessions, horses are very rarely taught the 'airs above the ground'. Fortunately, the Lipizzaner stallions came to Britain on a highly successful tour and I was able to photograph them again at Wembley during one of their gala performances.

When watching the Spanish Riding School of Vienna, one can't help but feel what an important part of Austria's history the school represents. Its aims are

(Far left) Seventeen-year-old Portuguese rider Carlos Couneiro trains with Luis Valença at his establishment in Vila Franca, north of Lisbon. Luis Valença is a member of the Portuguese School of Equestrian Art whose main objective is to keep the traditions of the classical dressage methods alive.

(Left) Portuguese School of Equestrian Art.

to maintain the classical art of riding, to pass such skills on to future generations and to train the noble Lipizzaner stallions to perfection. The school sees it as its duty to ensure the long-term future of the world's last baroque horse. The school also claims to be the

breed of horse to execute the most difficult exercises in perfect balance. This is achieved largely by gymnastic training and finds expression in the perfect harmony of apparently effortless, yet exceptionally difficult movements. The classical jumps or 'airs above

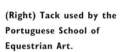

(Right) Tack used by the Portuguese School of Equestrian Art.

(Far right) Eleito, a Lusitano stallion, being long-reined, England 1997.
  This long-reining picture was taken at Chapel House Farm, Okewood Hill, Surrey. Eleito is a pure-bred Lusitano stallion. In 1989 he was Champion of Champions at Colega, the annual celebration of Lusitano stallions.

only one in the world where classical horsemanship is still cultivated in its purest form.

  The name of the Spanish Riding School dates back as far as 1572 and derives from the fact that only horses of Spanish origin – namely the Lipizzaner stallions – have been trained in *haute école* since the school's foundation. Their exceptional qualities of strength, intelligence and nobility make the Lipizzaner especially suitable for this work. The term '*haute école* of equitation' is synonymous with the ability of this

the ground', such as the levade, the capriole, and the courbette, demonstrate this principle. They are drawn from natural movements and are developed in training. This renders the horse so supple that he can shift without effort from a state of intense concentration to one of total relaxation.

  In the sixteenth century, under Emperor Charles VI, the Imperial Riding School was used for the education and instruction of young noblemen and for the training of horses for *haute école* and combat.

Today the Spanish Riding School of Vienna aims to safeguard the original principles of equestrian art and to demonstrate those in public performances.

The school also strives to exercise a general influence on the art of dressage by training disciples. The classical principles are now accepted by the FEI (Fédération Equestre Internationale) and throughout the world. The school also sets out to control the breeding of the Lipizzaner by using only those stallions who have proved their dexterity for *haute école*.

Immediately after my stay in Vienna, I travelled to Lisbon to witness how the Portuguese School of Equestrian Art keep their equestrian tradition alive. I had seen the Iberian horses that the Portuguese call Lusitanos before, but seeing this breed in their own setting at the Queluz Palace, where the school is presently based, was very impressive indeed. There is a certain calmness about the place, and the way the riders of the school work with their horses instilled a feeling of nobility. Nothing seems to faze this remarkable breed which has existed in the south-east of the Iberian Peninsula for many thousands of years. I was astonished to notice that during their gala performance, held at Queluz every Wednesday, there was a constant, noisy coming and going of visitors, none of which seemed to unsettle the Lusitanos in the slightest. Seeing the stallions again one evening during a show performance in torrential rain only enforced my sentiment that this breed is most definitely exceptional! Not only does the Lusitano have all the physical qualities needed for the required movements, but generosity and kindness literally ooze through his

A Portuguese bullfighter
on his horse during an
evening session in Lisbon's
Campo Pequeno on the
Praça de Touros. This shot
was taken on a very slow
shutter speed to enhance
the movement.

body. Needless to say, the entire audience felt an overwhelming sense of compassion for the riders and horses who bravely soldiered on. The applause nearly brought the house down.

Talking to the present director of the school, Guilherme Borba, I learned that, in Portugal, the Court Riding Academy existed until 1807, when it was closed as a result of the Napoleonic Wars. Despite its closure for many years, its teaching and tradition have been maintained and have never failed to influence riding techniques in Portugal where the style has always remained alive. It was thanks to equestrian bullfighting, an eminent Portuguese event cultivated by monarchs and aristocrats, that Portuguese riders maintained not only an authentic and refined artistic taste, but also the same type of horse, the same style of riding and the same costumes and tack that the royal stables used in the eighteenth century. The riding academy of the Portuguese Court was closed in the nineteenth century but, fortunately, its tradition was never extinguished and has never failed to influence the style of riding in Portugal.

The Escola Portuguesa de Arte Equestre was founded in 1979 by the Ministry of Agriculture. It set out to be a continuation of what was the Royal Riding Stable.

Some of the school's riders have their own yards where they train Lusitanos on the same classical principles. Luis Valença, for example, has beautiful facilities in Vila Franca, 40 minutes' drive north of Lisbon. He organises marvellous displays on site as well as touring around the world with his show. When

I went to Luis's establishment his daughter Luisa was kind enough to let her fabulous grey partner Zagalo run free in the bullring so that I could take some photographs.

One evening I went to see some bullfighting at Lisbon's Campo Pequeno. The Praça de Touros is a most fabulous arena, built in red brick. Walking around the building I was amazed at how relaxed and almost laid back the riders and horses seemed to be. The public had free access to the horses and could watch, or even talk to, the riders while they were warming up. Both the Lusitanos and their riders were immaculately turned out and bore a most noble air.

I had never attended a bullfight before and felt a mixture of excitement, anticipation and worry as to whether I was going to enjoy it. The build up until the moment when the first bull actually entered the arena was tremendous. The minute that horse, rider and bull all shared the middle of the arena, I couldn't help but feel a very strong atmosphere of nobleness, mutual respect and dignity. The horses were beautifully schooled and responded elegantly and effortlessly to the riders' commands. Although the aim is to tire the bull, not to kill it, I felt that a sense of pride and dignity always remained.

I also travelled to Jerez de la Frontera, where Alvaro Domecq founded a classical riding school with pure-bred Andalusians. Unfortunately, due to internal political problems, I was not allowed to photograph at the school where Alvaro Domecq is, in fact, no longer director. He was, none the less, kind enough to invite me to his farm where I watched a training session of young Andalusian horses who were being schooled for the bullring. Most of the movements the bullfighter teaches his Andalusian horse are featured in classical movements such as passage, piaffe, pirouette or half pass. I was fascinated by the lightness and ease with which the Andalusian horse responded to the slightest aids. Although I was very disappointed at having been refused access to the school itself, I must say that watching Alvaro Domecq and his fellow *rejoneadors* (bullfighters on horseback) at work was a worthwhile compensation.

Finally, I visited the Cadre Noir of Saumur in France. There I encountered similar internal political issues as in Spain. Not that I wasn't allowed access, in fact I was given written confirmation months before my visit. No, it was due to the bureaucracy of this institution that I had to spend two gloriously sunny days talking to various people, including Monsieur Christian Cambo, Director of the Ecole Nationale d'Equitation and Monsieur le Colonel Carde, *Ecuyer en Chef* (Chief Rider) of the Cadre Noir before riders and horses were finally organised for a photo call. The major difficulty in Saumur is that the Cadre Noir is integrated into the National Riding School – Ecole Nationale d'Equitation. That in itself wouldn't be such a drama, however, M. Cambo, the overall chief, is a civilian, while Colonel Carde is an army officer. Have you ever come across an officer who likes receiving orders from a civilian?

My frustration reached an uncomfortable level once I noticed that the weather had turned by the time les Messieurs Ecuyers du Cadre Noir were ready

for me. Grey and overcast skies replaced the fabulous autumn colours for which the Loire valley is so famous. Being a dedicated photographer doesn't come without its testing moments!

That aside, I am particularly pleased with a photograph of one of the riders in front of the magnificent castle of Saumur! Furthermore, my meetings with M. Cambo and Colonel Carde were not totally in vain because both informed me about the origins and aims of the school and the Cadre Noir itself.

The origins of the school in Saumur can be traced back as far as the sixteenth century when King Henry IV gave Saumur to his friend Duplese-Mornay who founded a Protestant university with a riding academy. In 1763, King Louis XV gave orders to reorganise the French Cavalry. 'The nicest riding school in the world' was then built on the Chardonnet to welcome the cavalry officers, and it stayed in service until 1788, just before the French Revolution. From 1789 to 1814 there was no time to cultivate the equestrian art but on Christmas Eve 1814, King Louis XVIII created L'Ecole d'Instruction des Troupes à Cheval in Saumur. It was then re-established under the name of Ecole Royale de Cavalerie in 1824. It included a military and an academic manège in which military riding principles were taught. And it

was there that the *haute école* was officially cultivated. Under Louis Philippe I the riders changed the colour of their uniform to the black we are used to nowadays and the name 'Cadre Noir' was given to the riding instructors of the cavalry school.

As for the doctrine, the *Ecuyer en Chef* explained that the aim of academic equitation is to allow the horse to regain the graceful movements he had before being broken in. To achieve this, the horse is trained using exercises that make him progressively more supple and obedient to the rider's aids. In 1814 the riders called on the traditions of Versailles. Later, General L'Hotte enriched French tradition and provided it with a style of its own.

The airs above the ground appeared during the Italian Renaissance and were used to improve the choreography of the carousel. Those movements were considered necessary to the education of the students and were practised without stirrups. The courbette and croupade have been retained in a style particular to Saumur. The capriole, however, keeps its classical style.

I hope that the following pages of pictures and the extensive interview with the First *Oberbereiter* of the Spanish Riding School of Vienna, Arthur Kottas-Heldenberg, will capture your imagination to the same extent as it did mine.

(Far left) Eleito, a Lusitano stallion, being long-reined, England 1997.

(Left) Francisco Bessa de Carvalho resting his hand on the Lusitano stallion Eleito before entering the arena for his long-reining display, England 1997.

Arthur Kottas-Heldenberg

Arthur Kottas-Heldenberg, First *Oberbereiter* (chief rider) of the Spanish Riding School, found his way into the saddle even before he started primary school. This doesn't come as a huge surprise because not only was his grandfather an accomplished and famous horseman but his parents owned the oldest riding school in Vienna. Although Arthur showed some interest in other sports, his mother warned him that skiing and ice skating were far too dangerous and that he would be much safer on the back of a horse. When Arthur was in his early teens a family friend, Mrs Savera, gave him some of her horses to ride. They proved to be excellent schoolmasters on whom Arthur, at the age of twelve and thirteen, won two consecutive junior dressage titles. The foundation of his fascination with the art of dressage was laid. However, Arthur admits that he 'found dressage far too difficult' and that he 'hugely enjoyed show jumping, especially as show jumpers were hailed as successful riders far quicker'.

Arthur's father wanted him to work in his grandfather's haulage company. However, being a 'little rebel' and having had some of the riders of the Spanish Riding School who saw him ride say, 'If you don't know what to do with yourself once you have finished school, come and join us,' Arthur's mind was firmly made up and a career in the world's most famous school of classical riding seemed inevitable. It was in 1960, at the age of fifteen, that Arthur joined the Spanish Riding School as an *élève* (apprentice) under the leadership of Colonel Alois Podhajsky. Asked

which rider influenced him most, Arthur was quick to point out that: 'All the *Bereiters* and *Oberbereiters* have been great teachers, particularly Chief *Oberbereiter-Bereiter* Georg Wahl who was my trainer for seven years.' Every *Bereiter* or *Oberbereiter* of the Spanish Riding School has the task of taking an apprentice under his wing.

It was as early as 1964, only four years after he joined the school, that Arthur's career took an impressive step forward.

'The school was scheduled to tour the USA but we encountered a huge problem. Two of our riders had been involved in a horrific car crash in Portugal.

(Right) Arthur Kottas-Heldenberg, First *Oberbereiter* of the Spanish Riding School, Vienna.

(Far right) Lipizzaner stallion performing a courbette in hand. This is one of the most difficult leaps of the airs above the ground. The horse raises its forefeet, as for the levade, then takes several leaps forward on its hind legs without lowering its front legs.

Oberbereiter Irbinger was badly injured and *Bereiter* Riedler was killed. It was therefore imperative to quickly match up their horses with the right riders. They were specifically looking to find someone who could ride the capriole. No one got as much out of this particular horse as I did and so I was chosen to join the US tour as an apprentice to perform the ridden capriole. From that moment on the capriole has become my speciality and I perform it to date. In fact, every rider specialises in a particular movement of the airs above the ground but has the expertise to teach the horses all the different jumps.'

At nineteen, Arthur was the youngest apprentice ever to ride in a dress performance. 'Usually apprentices only ride in the young stallions section. Later, generally after four to six years, they are given the chance to ride in the quadrille because it is the stepping stone to being nominated as *Bereiter-Anwärter* (rider candidate). This is a big step and one is given a horse to school up to the equivalent of Grand Prix level, ready for a dress performance. After having passed a theoretical exam on the horse as well as on general education, one is appointed *Bereiter* (rider). The best *Bereiters* will make it to *Oberbereiter-Bereiter*. And if one is a very good *Oberbereiter-Bereiter*, one gets selected to become the First *Oberbereiter-Bereiter*.' Arthur was the youngest ever *Oberbereiter-Bereiter* before reaching the highest level of all in 1995.

As First *Oberbereiter* Arthur is responsible for the entire course of events at the school, which means that he is expected to know everything. 'I see it as a big challenge because I get confronted with new

things on a daily basis. Further, I feel that being a member of the Spanish Riding School is a unique privilege. Our school is the last riding institution in which the art of classical riding is taught and shown in its purest form. To be part of this is tremendous. It is the wish of many, yet only a few actually make it. And to then be elected First *Oberbereiter*, well, this can only be achieved by one person at the time!'

Arthur has been part of this unequalled experience for 37 years and there has not been one single day when he thought that he might have been better off doing something else. 'I would stay in the Spanish Riding School even if I won millions in the lottery!'

Similar to international competition riders, the riders of the Spanish Riding School strive for perfection in every performance that they give. 'To ride in a dress performance is special and it is not infrequent that we see people in the audience being moved to tears. I often receive letters from old or sick people whose last wish it is to attend one of our performances. It is a remarkable feeling knowing that we are capable of fulfilling people's last wishes. Knowing that all our performances have the potential of being a special day for someone does put the pressure on.'

Again, the comparison to riding in a competition can be drawn because every performance is a real thrill. This excitement is accentuated by the fact that success does not depend on only one rider. 'At a show, alone, one rider and his horse are judged. With us it's down to a collective performance and a chain is only as strong as its weakest link. We are therefore accustomed to give our best so that we remain a member of the performing team. Age or experience doesn't necessarily get you into the team. If a younger rider shows better form, the older rider will have to stay on the bench. We are all pushed to give one hundred per cent.'

The atmosphere among the riders is, however, kept in balance. 'Of course there is a healthy rivalry among the riders because they all want to get to the top and it is my duty as First *Oberbereiter* to find the right reason for who is going to be left out. It is my task to decide on who will make the team.'

After every performance the riders assemble to discuss each part of the show. 'The rider who stayed on the bench makes notes on each section and, together with the stable manager, we all sit down to evaluate our performance so that we can, if necessary, adjust things for the next presentation.'

Ridden work at the Spanish Riding School starts as early as seven in the morning. From seven to ten, young horses are lunged, apprentices receive their tuition and horses which need specific help are seen to. From ten o'clock to twelve the paying public is let in to observe the training. 'It is important to work in peace for a few hours. After all, not many riders tolerate an audience while training. We are very open because we have nothing to hide and we are happy to attract more than a thousand people on every working day. The Spanish Riding School appeals to people from all over the world and is one of the biggest attractions Austria offers. We feel we are ambassadors of our country.'

Its popularity is primarily due to the importance the Spanish Riding School places on keeping the

Arthur Kottas-Heldenberg, First *Oberbereiter* of the Spanish Riding School, Vienna performing a capriole on the 24-year-old Lipizzaner stallion Siglavi Britanica during a rehearsal at Wembley. In 1964 the Spanish Riding School was specifically looking for a rider who could perform the capriole to join their US tour following the tragic death of *Bereiter* Riedler. Arthur, still an apprentice at the time, got the best out of the horse in question. From that moment on the capriole became his speciality. 'When schooling young horses we always try to spot those who might show an aptitude for a movement above the ground. When we find a horse with the right temperament and ability we try to complete and refine the movement.'

ancient tradition of the art of classical riding alive.

'There are many forms of riding. The classical way, however, reaches back centuries and has proved to be the right one. When following it, one realises that it is a very open way of schooling. It is a wide road that accommodates every horse.

'One of its most important characteristics is to ask the horse but never to demand too much. Only when a rider has himself under control can he control the horse. My advice is take time but don't waste it. I am only following the right path when I have trained my horse physically and psychologically for it to carry out what I have asked from it.

'Many paths lead to Rome; you only have to find the one that is right for you. I have picked a cherry out of every rider's basket; for example, the industriousness of *Oberbereiter* Lauscher and the correct giving of the aids of *Oberbereiter-Bereiter* Georg Wahl. But I never attempted to copy just one in particular because I didn't want to be a bad replica. When one is surrounded by so many excellent horsemen, something is bound to rub off. Furthermore, if you don't try, you

don't get any answers. So far I have always received an answer.'

Equally important in completing the image of classical dressage in Vienna is the Lipizzaner. 'It is a baroque horse and we see it as one of our duties to preserve this culture for many generations to come. The Lipizzaner is a strong horse, sturdy, intelligent and industrious. His movements are unique. The Lipizzaner has a high knee action and therefore less extension but offers a great deal of advantages in his collection.'

Every horse has his own personality and the Lipizzaner is no exception to the rule. 'They are all different and we have to accept, as with every horse, that some might have weaknesses. It is our duty as riders to come to terms with possible shortcomings and to find a way to maximise every horse's potential.'

When it comes to airs above the ground, some Lipizzaner horses make better 'jumpers' than others. Nevertheless, each horse is also trained to work on the flat. 'The really talented jumpers, however, are kept as specialists because asking them to perform in other areas as well would be too demanding for them.'

The airs above the ground can be traced back to the battlefields of the Middle Ages. 'In defence the knights had their horses lash out behind. As protection against the opponent's lance, horses were asked to do the levade. To be on the attack and yet be protected they let their horses jump forward standing up on their hind legs. We have merely refined those movements.'

A further point that is stressed within the ideology of the art of classical riding is that trainers never ask for unnatural movements. 'As trainers we make sure never to go against nature. The movements that we teach and that we try to achieve are typical movements that we simply try to perfect and refine. You won't see a horse do one-time flying changes in the field but you will notice horses changing leads when galloping around, doing piaffe or passage when they are excited and the levade when they are playing. Horses are showing us their power and we must try to utilise their strength and school them accordingly. The training should show a harmony between horse and rider. All that is harmonious is beautiful. All that is done with ease is beautiful. Therefore, every rider's aim must surely be to present the most difficult exercise with ease.'

Another point Arthur is determined to put across is that feeling alone is not enough. A rider has to use his mind. 'A rider has to be able to judge whether a horse is physically and mentally strong enough to carry out what it has been asked for. In this way a horse will never get into a stressful situation. It is so important to ask oneself: "If the horse could talk and I was to ask it whether it actually knows what I want from it, would it reply, 'No idea!' or 'Yes, of course I do. I'm just not quite strong enough yet.'" I have never wanted to have a subservient horse. Horses are individuals. I accept them for what they are. It's similar to a child. I wouldn't ask a child with short legs to become a basketball player. I have to recognise the horse's capabilities. No horse is capable of doing everything.'

In Arthur's mind, there is no such thing as a complete rider. 'To be a good rider, one has to have

Arthur Kottas-Heldenberg, First *Oberbereiter*, performing passage and piaffe between the pillars on the fourteen-year-old stallion Favory Plutona during a morning training session at Vienna's Hofburg, the home of the Spanish Riding School. Between ten and noon the paying public is allowed to watch the schooling sessions of the Lipizzaner stallions. 'Favory Plutona has a marvellous character and a lot of ability. He could feature in all the different parts of our programme other than the airs above the ground. However, I ride him in the pas de deux. Being one of our finest stallions he regularly returns to our stud in Piber for breeding.'

lived at least two lives because one lifetime surely wouldn't be enough! No matter what discipline, for me there are only two types of riders, good ones and bad ones!'

When asked to define his riding strength, Arthur believes that most of his success is due to his temperament. 'I am ninety-five per cent in control and think that I have a great deal of feeling for horse and rider.'

Nevertheless, the First *Oberbereiter* of the Spanish Riding School would welcome more recognition from

Austrian riders. 'The appreciation is unquestionable. However, some Austrian riders believe that we are terrific on Lipizzaner horses but think that we are not as good as them because we don't compete at shows. There is a good reason for that. To be a *Bereiter* of the Spanish Riding School is a task for life. We don't only ride during the performances, we train our horses from scratch. Besides, I am sure that on the right horse any of our riders would achieve an outstanding result internationally.'

Arthur is also a keen teacher/trainer outside of his duties at the Spanish Riding School. Not only does he have his own yard where he trains his two daughters plus other people and their horses, he also goes abroad regularly. 'I love teaching and I am very fond of England where I do the Training Teachers of Tomorrow (TTT) clinic.'

He takes the principles of the classical method wherever he goes and finds conveying a belief he is convinced of very satisfying. 'Riding the classical way means to truly demand the right thing at the right moment. However long the teaching process takes, I will have the assurance that the lesson has been taught and therefore learned correctly. In the classical way we have to pay attention to the natural freedom of movement of the horse. The walk has to have a correct four beats, the legs have to move diagonally at the trot and the canter has to have three beats. In training we then try to improve the gaits and encourage the horse to reach his peak performance. One has to understand the horse and the horse has to understand the rider. I have to believe in what I do and I can't do the opposite to what I preach. The rider's discipline and sense of fairness are eminent. It is crucial not to look for the mistakes in others, but to admit that it might not be my day. On such days I will demand less of my horse and hope for a better tomorrow.'

The classical method demands consistency in the training of horse and rider. Furthermore, the rider has to keep his cool at all times. Arthur is quick to emphasise that 'a person has the possibility to contradict, a horse, however, can only resist'. It is therefore the rider's obligation to know why a horse resists. Is it because I have asked too much? Have I asked in a wrong way? Or has the horse misunderstood me? The language we use is through our seat, our legs and our hands. A good rider has to have a feeling for the horse and think like a horse. Only then has he got his horse under control.'

Arthur's final comment about horsemanship is that 'Women are better riders than most men because they are generally more sensitive. For the secret is not only to love horses but to have the ability to understand them.'

Oberbereiter Klaus Krzisch schooling Siglavi Mantua during a morning session in the Hofburg. Klaus joined the Spanish Riding School as an apprentice at the age of fifteen and worked his way up to become a chief rider in 1990. He has been riding at the school for 33 years. 'Getting into the school is not very difficult. It's staying on which can be tricky! Yes, there have been moments when I thought I couldn't cope. The training of horses and riders can be so very challenging! It's just a matter of learning and persevering. One can't really seek help because, at the end of the day, it's only down to oneself. The idea is to find your own path to success.'

Oberbereiter Klaus Krzisch and the eighteen-year-old stallion Siglavi Mantua accompanied the Spanish Riding School on their 1997 tour of Britain. The pair are pictured showing their unparalleled skills in solo performance. 'Siglavi Mantua has a marvellous character. I would give him only the highest marks! He has been very easy to train and started to perform in "the steps and movements of the classical school" section of our programme from the age of seven. Three years on he was chosen for the solo act and we have been performing it together for eleven years now! Hopefully Siglavi Mantua will perform for another five to six years. He has such a fantastic attitude. Nothing fazes him, not the spotlight, not the cameras and certainly not the crowd!

'As for me, I have been riding at the Spanish Riding School for thirty-three years. Although I don't have a horsy background, I have always had a love of animals. As it happens, I tried horses and just stuck with them. Being around horses is just such fun and a great deal more fulfilling then working with people. I just couldn't imagine being stuck in an office. What makes being here so special is the horses and working to keep the traditions of the classical training method alive. I can't conceive of having a better job!'

Bereiter Wolfgang Eder joined the Spanish Riding School of Vienna as an apprentice in 1974. He was born into a horse-loving family and started to ride at the age of six. Wolfgang enjoys going on tour with the Spanish Riding School and finds representing the school, its riding traditions and Austria hugely fulfilling. In this picture Wolfgang is performing piaffe on fifteen-year-old Maestoso Morella during a morning session at Vienna's Hofburg. 'Maestoso has a very strong character. I can't just demand things of him. I have to keep him happy and train him in a playful way. I can't impose anything on him. If he resists I'm better off leaving him and trying again the following day.'

Bereiter Andreas Harrer and Neapolitano Nima I performing a levade during rehearsals on the 1997 British Tour of the Spanish Riding School. Andreas joined the Spanish Riding School of Vienna at the age of eighteen and has been a member of the team for 25 years. It was after seeing a performance of the Spanish Riding School that Andreas was inspired to apply for a post. 'Many people tried to talk me out of it. However, I can be a bit stubborn and as I had set my heart on trying to apply I just went for it! Although it can be tough as an apprentice, I have never regretted my decision. Yes, there are hard moments but they are subjective. The highs helped me to overcome the lows. After rain there is sunshine!

'Neapolitano Nima I has a very strong character. His strength is the affinity we share. He likes working. We realised that he had an aptitude for the levade during the work in hand. He found the collection under saddle rather difficult. Neapolitano Nima I is nineteen now and only performs levade and piaffe between the pilars. He is truly a good buddy and very reliable. However, I have to show him his boundaries. Within those borders I can let him move freely.'

Bereiter Andreas Hausberger and Conversano Isabella performing their long-rein routine at a gala performance of the Spanish Riding School during their 1997 tour of Britain. Andreas grew up with horses in the south of Austria where his parents have a stud farm. He has always had a great love of animals. Andreas joined the Spanish Riding School of Vienna as an apprentice fourteen years ago at the relatively advanced age of nineteen.

'I applied three years in a row to join but, unfortunately, there was never a place available. I had almost given up hope when, out of the blue, I was asked to come for an interview. I rode in front of a panel and to my delight I was accepted. My childhood dream had finally come true! However, the training at the school is very tough. I remember riding with sore and bruised knees for a whole year! To succeed one has to be very strong mentally. Like in every walk of life, there are moments when obstacles seem impassable.

'As apprentices we are all given young stallions to bring on to Grand Prix level. Conversano Isabella was entrusted to me as a three and a half year old. We grew together and know each other inside out! When he was four I rode him in the young stallions' section. Then he went in the quadrille for three years. When he was familiar with all the movements we tried long-reining him. He showed a great talent and had all the right characteristics for the job. Conversano Isabella is very intelligent. He has a very sensitive mouth, is extremely alert and listens to my voice. However, he can also be mischievous at times! When he is a bit too fresh I usually ride him before the performance and then he is as good as gold. Although we both started off as inexperienced and green individuals, it was thanks to my work with Conversano Isabella that I became a *Bereiter* in 1993. The work with horses is so fascinating! I am still overwhelmed every time I enter our riding school in Vienna! I would describe my work as a dream job!'

A Lipizzaner and rider from
the Spanish Riding School
of Vienna.

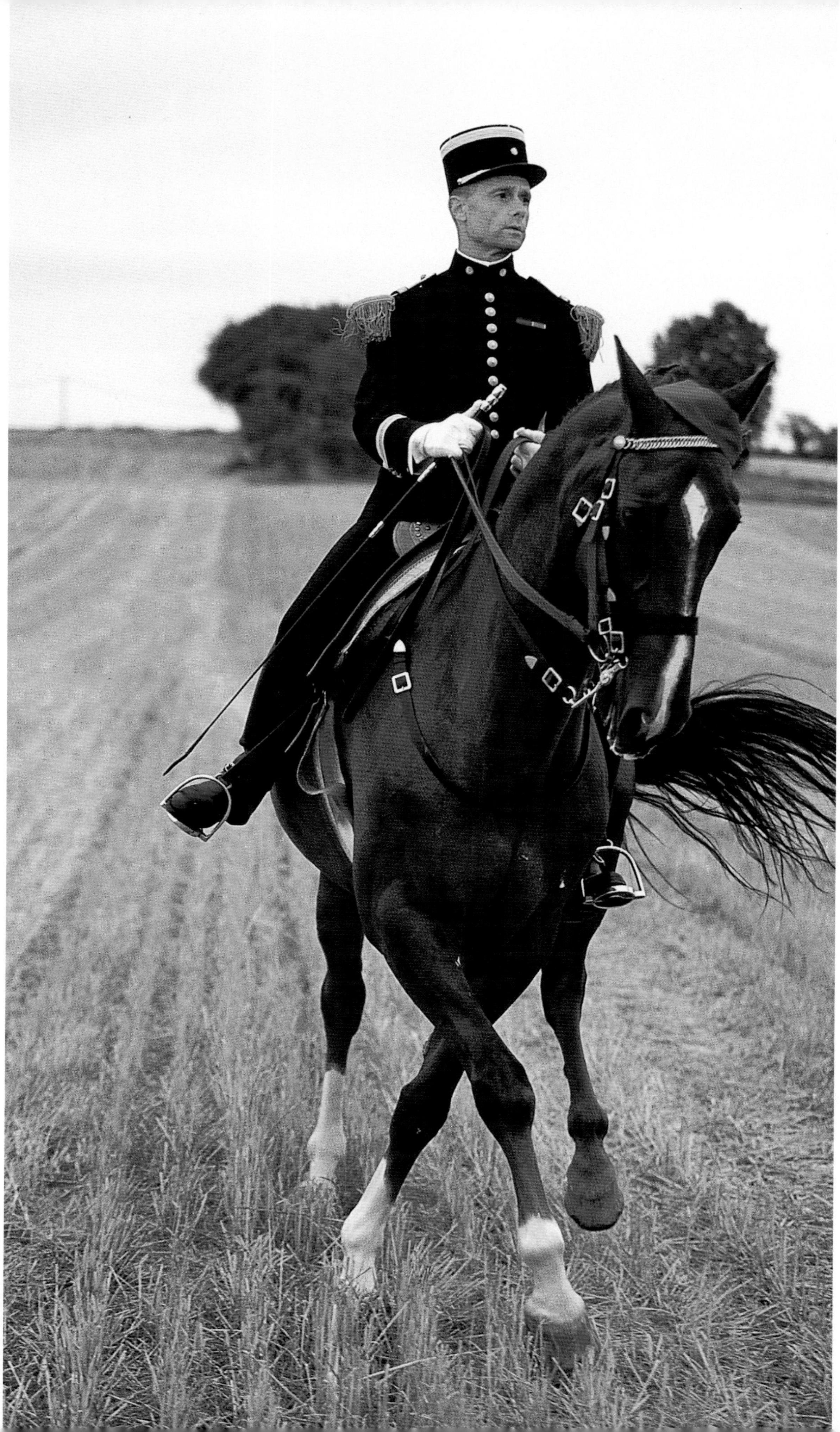

Jean-Louis Guntz joined the Cadre Noir of Saumur at the age of twenty at a time when the institution was still purely a military school. The biggest difference between the Cadre Noir and the other institutions of classical dressage is that the horses of the Cadre Noir are not all of the same breed. Although they have to be French-bred, Rubis de Ruyer, for example, the horse on which Jean-Louis is pictured here, is half Thoroughbred and half Trotter. As Jean Louis explains: 'It is probably not the best of pedigrees! But, thanks to Rubis de Ruyer's goodwill, big heart and generous attitude, I managed to train him to Grand Prix level fairly easily. I started riding him as a four year old and by the age of seven he knew all the movements.'

As well as being a rider (ecuyer) of the Cadre Noir, Jean-Louis also competes in international dressage competitions. Horses have always been his passion. He started off in racing and found it 'the most fascinating and purest of all equestrian disciplines'. He says, 'Dressage is the most refined activity of them all and as a rider I needed to develop a high level of animal psychology to succeed in it. However, if there happened to be a fence in the middle of the dressage arena, I would be in heaven!'

Jean-Louis is very humble about his achievements and believes that: 'It is only by having a good horse that one becomes a good rider because one derives so much pleasure from it.'

He adds, 'There is no such thing as knowing a horse. Riding allows me to discover more about my horse each day. I might set out to do a specific lesson with a horse but what is so fascinating is that it is impossible to predict his reactions. It is very difficult to be sure of what a horse is prepared to offer us. And what he does offer us is rarely what we had expected; it is always something new! Riding allows me to distance myself from life's daily occurrences. When I am on a horse I forget everything else. I am absorbed by what I do. It is a certain escapism. When sitting on a horse my mind reaches a higher plane, especially when walking on a loose rein! When schooling a horse I give myself completely. I only think about what is happening under my saddle. Does the horse give himself, does he resist or does he co-operate?'

By joining the Cadre Noir as *sous ecuyer*, Capitaine Pierre de Bastard has fulfilled his childhood dream. He started his career at the military school in Fontainebleau where he acquired his military rank. His second love is three day eventing. Pierre loves Britain and has competed at Blenheim and at Bramham where he came second in 1996. De Bastard specialises in the movements above the ground. Here he is pictured performing a courbette on an eighteen-year-old Selle Français, Milord Sylvannais. 'Working with the "jumpers" (*sauteurs*) is a blend of show jumping, because the preparation is similar, and three day eventing, because there is, nevertheless, an element of danger. The "jumper" can lose his balance and fall. The movements have to be done very quickly. They are very energetic and yet very supple. They have to be performed with lightness and not force.

'I enjoy performing and working as part of a team. It's fun to ride the jumpers and hear the cheers of the spectators! I do get angry at myself when I mess up a movement. I have the desire to do it better next time and I feel enormous joy when it all goes well! The capriole is the most difficult of movements. The timing is crucial. One can only ask for it the very second the horse is in perfect balance. When you find the moment it is magic, like jumping a very big fence! The Cadre Noir is a magnificent institution. We are dressed in a fabulous uniform and have the pleasure of preserving the French tradition of classical dressage.'

(Right) João Filipe de Figueiredo, chief rider of the Portuguese School of Equestrian Art, in full extended trot with a fourteen-year-old Lusitano stallion, Baú, from the Alter Real Stud during a performance at the Queluz Palace.

(Far right) João Filipe de Figueiredo about to do a canter pirouette on Baú during their solo performance at the palace in Queluz. Like most riders of the Portuguese School of Equestrian Art, João Filipe does not spend his entire day at the school. He is also a practicing vet.

Pedro Viotty of the Portuguese School of Equestrian Art rehearsing the levade in hand with the Lusitano stallion Hexodo minutes before the beginning of the dress performance at the Queluz Palace.

(Above) Francisco Bessa de Carvalho performing a levade
during a performance of the Portuguese School of Equestrian
Art at the Queluz Palace.

(Right) Francisco Bessa de Carvalho working the Lusitano
stallion Casto in hand during a performance of the
Portuguese School of Equestrian Art at the Queluz Palace.

(Left) Putting the final touches to a horse's tail before
performing airs above the ground.

Nuno Palma Santos and the Lusitano stallion Fúxico in perfect harmony. All the stallions used at the Portuguese School of Equestrian Art are Lusitanos bred at the Alter Real Stud.

(Left) Nuno Palma Santos in passage during the warm up before the dress performance at the Palace of Queluz.

Carlos Couneiro is seventeen years old and rides for Luis Valença at his establishment in Vila Franca, north of Lisbon. Carlos started performing in Luis Valença's shows in 1997. As well as touring the world, Luis organises numerous displays of classical dressage on his premises. It is quite breathtaking to witness the enthusiasm and lightness with which the Lusitano horse seems willingly to offer his natural movements to his rider.

Luis Domecq Domecq, nephew of Alvaro Domecq Romero, followed the Domecq tradition and performs as a mounted bullfighter (*rejoneador*). His bullfighting style is often compared to that of his grandfather, Alvaro Domecq y Diez. In performance Luis is elegant, highly skilled, majestic and full of passion. Despite his sobriety, audiences adore the excitement of his fighting style. He is full of courage and exudes tremendous self-confidence. When facing the bull, he gives his challenger every chance and his approach is logical, tactical and yet full of emotion. Luis is also a key figure in his uncle's new school of equestrian art.

(Far left) Here Luis is pictured in a session during which young bulls are selected. Only the finest breeding lines are chosen for the bullring. Luis is riding Duende, a highly skilled Andalusian on whom Luis has performed in the bullring on numerous occasions.

(Left) Kneeling down is Duque, a pure-bred Andalusian.

Zagalo, the fabulous grey partner of Luisa Valença, daughter of Luis Valença, running free in the bullring at his home in Vila Franca. Luisa and Zagalo usually perform a choreographed solo to music. They have performed over 900 times to the delight of spectators around the world.

Alvaro Domecq Romero, one of the world's most accomplished and charismatic horsemen, followed in his father's footsteps almost from the day he was born. Aged five, Alvaro won his first trophy at the horse fair in Seville. Two years on, he rode in his first bullfight. In 1960, at the age of twenty, he became a fully qualified mounted bullfighter (*rejoneador*) and received a highly coveted decoration from his father, Alvaro Domecq y Diez, during a memorable charity bullfight. Since then, Alvaro has delighted audiences in Spain, Portugal, France, Colombia, Venezuela, Ecuador and Mexico with his equestrian skills and distinctive courage. In 1985 and after 1544 bullfights, Alvaro finally left the bullring. However, together with his two nephews, Luis and Antonio, who are keeping the Domecq tradition alive, Alvaro trains horses and breeds bulls on his farm, Los Alburejos, near a small town called Medina Sidonia.

Here Alvaro is performing a pirouette on the Andalusian stallion Urdidor during a schooling session. In 1973 the King of Spain presented Alvaro with the most distinguished equestrian prize Spain has to offer, 'the Golden Horse Trophy'. The same year Alvaro founded the Royal Andalusian School of Equestrian Art in his home town of Jerez de la Frontera. Once the school was established, Alvaro also travelled the international dressage circuit. He won Grand Prix competitions in Belgium, Denmark, Germany and Spain. It is thanks to Alvaro's achievements that the Spanish pure bred has become so fashionable throughout Europe.

Alvaro left the Royal School of Equestrian Art for political reasons but has since established a new school. His objectives remain as pure as ever: promoting the splendour of Andalusian equestrian art and the Spanish horse. Appropriately, he named his show 'The Equestrian Magic of Alvaro Domecq'.

Alvaro Domecq Romero is undoubtedly a man of great passion who has truly dedicated his life to horses.

It was always clear to Antonio Domecq Domecq, younger brother of Luis Domecq Domecq, that he would follow in his uncle's footsteps. Here Antonio is pictured riding Giraldillo and carrying the *garocha* which is used for rounding up the bulls in the field. Giraldillo is one of Antonio's most advanced partners. Horse and rider are in perfect balance and harmony. When in the bullring Antonio is much more spirited than his brother. He is a tremendously instinctive rider and has a unique approach to bullfighting. He likes taking risks and keeps audiences on the edge of their seats by performing extraordinary movements in front of the bull. A great improviser, Antonio has a very lively style and enchants spectators throughout his fights. Antonio is a classically trained rider and, together with his brother, is a key figure in his uncle's new School of Andalusian Equestrian Art.

COMPETITION RIDERS

No matter whether it is performed in a competition or shown purely as a demonstration, dressage is at its best when horse and rider execute the most difficult movements with seeming ease and in perfect harmony. Just as in either of the other two Olympic equestrian disciplines, it is the free-flowing movement of the horse that makes dressage so very enjoyable to watch. For those who don't ride but who are, none the less, enthusiasts, it is also wonderful to imagine what a rider must be feeling when he or she is at one with their horse. Riders record that it is, indeed, a sensational feeling and some even go as far as admitting that obtaining such a harmonious relationship can move them to tears. The sensation evoked by a well-presented dressage test is probably similar to the feeling one gets when looking at any form of art. Whether it is a particularly beautiful painting or a wonderful theatrical performance, the experience undoubtedly affects people on an emotional level.

With equestrian disciplines, however, there is the added element of a living creature, the horse, which leads us into a further dimension. The horse in itself embodies immense presence, elegance and beauty. It is a creature which exudes power. Its spirit is so free and unspoiled that the riders can only respect these characteristics as true qualities.

The rider too has distinctions of his own which are neither lesser nor greater, just different. It is probably safe to say that most people are governed by their intellect. Good reasoning combined with sensitivity can be of great value to a rider when it comes to schooling a horse. Marrying the two components creates a very exciting and fascinating combination indeed!

It is wonderful to witness the control a rider has over his or her partner. It is a control that should never be abusive nor disrespectful, but one which allows the rider to contain the horse's energy and muscular tension up to the very moment when the dressage test demands its release. It is equally as beautiful to see how a horse will return to a more collected state without resisting his rider's authority. It is then that the mutual understanding between horse and rider, at the highest level of the sport, becomes simply poetry in motion. Some might even call it an electrifying experience.

In this chapter I have focused on dressage riders who have a highly developed competitive streak. Here I am dealing with international riders who travel the world with their horses to compete at the top level of their chosen sport in pursuit of both perfection and those eminently desirable awards that they so desperately want to pick up at championships.

The same principles of schooling along classical lines are used by trainers and competitors when educating their horses. However, competition fever

1992 Barcelona Olympics, good luck cards for Laura Fry (GB) and Quarryman.

(Left) German rider Monica Theodorescu in a reflective mood after doing well at the 1996 CDIO at Aachen, the German selection trials for the Atlanta Olympics. 'It is a quiet moment when I probably felt proud of Grunox and our result. It's quite possible that I was thinking about our test and what a good feeling Grunox had given me.'

and the pressure to win can sometimes tempt riders to rush horses through their formative years. Some competitors may not wish to acknowledge that many talented horses never make it to the top because they have set too fast a training programme. However, the fact is that, no matter how gifted they are, horses cannot be hurried through their basic training if they are to reach the top and stay there.

The leading riders are fully aware of these risks and therefore try to respect the individual needs of their partners. Some horses may learn and develop at a faster pace than others. The training of a dressage horse is very much tailored to the horse's personality, willingness and ability to learn. Correct training will transform horses into athletes. The horses will learn to carry themselves properly and their riders will notice an improvement in the span of the horse's natural movements.

From a photographer's point of view I know that when watching competitive dressage I am drawn to focus on those images that are most photogenic. Fortunately, they are also the classical, most difficult and most interesting movements, such as piaffe, passage, canter pirouette, extensions, and the half pass in canter and trot. Flying changes are also inspiring, especially if a horse's weight is truly transferred on to his hind legs, because this allows for a high and impressive crossing of the front legs which can make a fabulous picture. Capturing horses performing those movements to perfection is hugely satisfying. At the same time, it also gives the viewer a better understanding of what is physically demanded of the horse.

In photography one can break down certain movements into various segments and this can show the horse's strength as well as a possible weakness. The better the movement is performed, the easier it is to take a good picture! However, the timing still has to be spot on! This is true for dressage even more than when photographing show jumping or three day eventing because the dressage horse stays in his most photogenic position, such as a full extension, for example, for a mere fraction of a second! You have to follow as well as feel the horse's rhythm in order to anticipate the correct moment at which to release the shutter. For example, I often follow the horse through my lens for a few one-time flying changes before I spot the best one. By following the horse at all times, the chances of capturing the perfect moment are greater. It demands a high level of permanent concentration, especially if you are at a championship where almost every rider is of importance.

When photographing dressage my main interest is to show the elegance, the agility, the concentration and the harmony in which horse and rider perform their tests.

The following pages look at dressage from a sporting point of view rather than as the pure artform portrayed in Chapter One. Top international riders talk about their sport, their horses and why their greatest desire is to achieve near to perfect harmony when presenting themselves in front of a panel of judges.

The selection of photographs was made by looking at the various styles particular horse and rider combinations adopt while performing thoroughly demanding movements.

Since the fabulous achievements with her horse Corlandus, French rider Margit Otto-Crépin has found another wonderfully expressive horse in her grey gelding, Lucky Lord. They have represented France on numerous occasions. Here they are captured during a training session at the 1995 CDIO in Aachen.

'When I am schooling a horse, it's as if I was in a totally different world! I am so concentrated on feeling my horse. I want to be with him, almost inside of him, as opposed to just sitting on top of him. In training I can't perform the movements unless I really feel them. During the test, however, I have no choice. I have to perform them. I usually risk a lot when I am riding my tests. That's just the way I am. I don't do it consciously. It's just me. This makes up my character and this is the way I think and express myself.

'Lucky Lord has a super character. He is a real fighter. Compared to Corlandus he is easy to ride. However, compared to my two new stallions I would have to say that Lucky Lord is extremely sensitive which can make him a little difficult!'

Swiss dressage rider Christine Stückelberger is a true phenomenon! Over the years she has won no fewer than 25 medals at European and World Championships as well as at Olympic Games. Five of these were gold medals! Her most famous horses were Granat and Gaugin de Lully. At present Christine has another superb partner in the thirteen-year-old Westphalian stallion Aquamarin, a horse Christine has had since he was eight. Previously Aquamarin had been ridden by a big strong man who had taken him to Prix St Georges level.

Aquamarin is rather headstrong with a mind of his own which has been very visible on more than one occasion when he makes a fuss about not wanting to enter the arena. When watching Christine in Geneva during the CDI-W, I witnessed what many people had feared would happen eventually: Aquamarin and Christine were eliminated for not entering the arena within the time allowed! Needless to say, Christine was very disappointed.

'Aquamarin went so well during the warm up. I thought I was floating! He usually gives me a feeling that is truly difficult to describe. He is incredibly strong mentally. Being a stallion, once he has something in his head it's terribly difficult for me to change his mind. He does notice my weaknesses and if he'd rather stay with his stable mate than enter the arena, I can only deal with him by being kind. Usually I dismount and lead him in. In Geneva nothing worked. He simply wanted to go back to his stable mate! He is a horse that needs a lot of attention and kindness. He is lovely to work with. He is such a willing horse who always wants to give you one hundred per cent in his work. Entering the arena, however, is a real thriller. I never know whether we'll actually make it! It's not that I am nervous about it. In fact, being calm at all times is my biggest strength. Once we're in the arena I know that he'll be wonderful. His strengths are his beauty and his elasticity, being loose. He is like a rubber ball. His canter is fantastic. He has tremendous presence and is hugely expressive in all his movements.

'When I first got Aquamarin he was uncontrollable. It took me a whole year before I could do anything with him. We had to start from scratch before he started to accept me. He had been ridden with a lot of force. I only weigh forty-seven kilos and am one hundred times weaker than Aquamarin! He had to understand that I am actually still sitting on his back and that I would like to say something! It all boils down to finding the right degree of understanding for one another. Aquamarin needs a lot of personal contact. At a show, you'll never see me sitting in the stands because I am always in the stable keeping him company. He demands that! One can never be rough with him. Our understanding is based on friendliness. Aquamarin is a miracle! He is very noble and knows how beautiful he is. He is very self-assured but deep down extremely sensitive.'

During the 1997 European Championships the pair were placed seventeenth and, as Christine explains, she was most disappointed with the judges' marks. 'I have the feeling that the judges are simply not giving Aquamarin the right marks. I am just not "in" at the moment. I really don't know why but they are definitely putting the brakes on. It can be quite frustrating at times. One either has to give up or try again. However, I do find the whole thing rather sad. I can live with the disappointment because Aquamarin is a young horse. He is still in the making

and not really well known at Grand Prix level. We therefore have to work our way up. Every rider knows that it takes two years before the judges accept a new partnership. It was no different when I rode Granat! It takes two years before the judges understand that you have a good horse. I believe that a horse that has been placed tenth various times can suddenly have a great moment. Just as a top rider can have a bad day. Why does the top rider who made a few little mistakes win? Why can't the best rider on the day win? However, I do know how difficult it is to stay objective. I am a judge myself.'

Christine says that sitting on Aquamarin is like being on a turbo-charged horse. 'He is a horse that always wants to go. That in itself is a wonderful feeling. Yes, it's difficult to control him. We are on the limit during each test but this is a challenge to me. I wouldn't like a horse that I'd have to push permanently. I prefer difficult horses. I want to ride with feeling and not with force. I'd rather stop riding than have to use strength!'

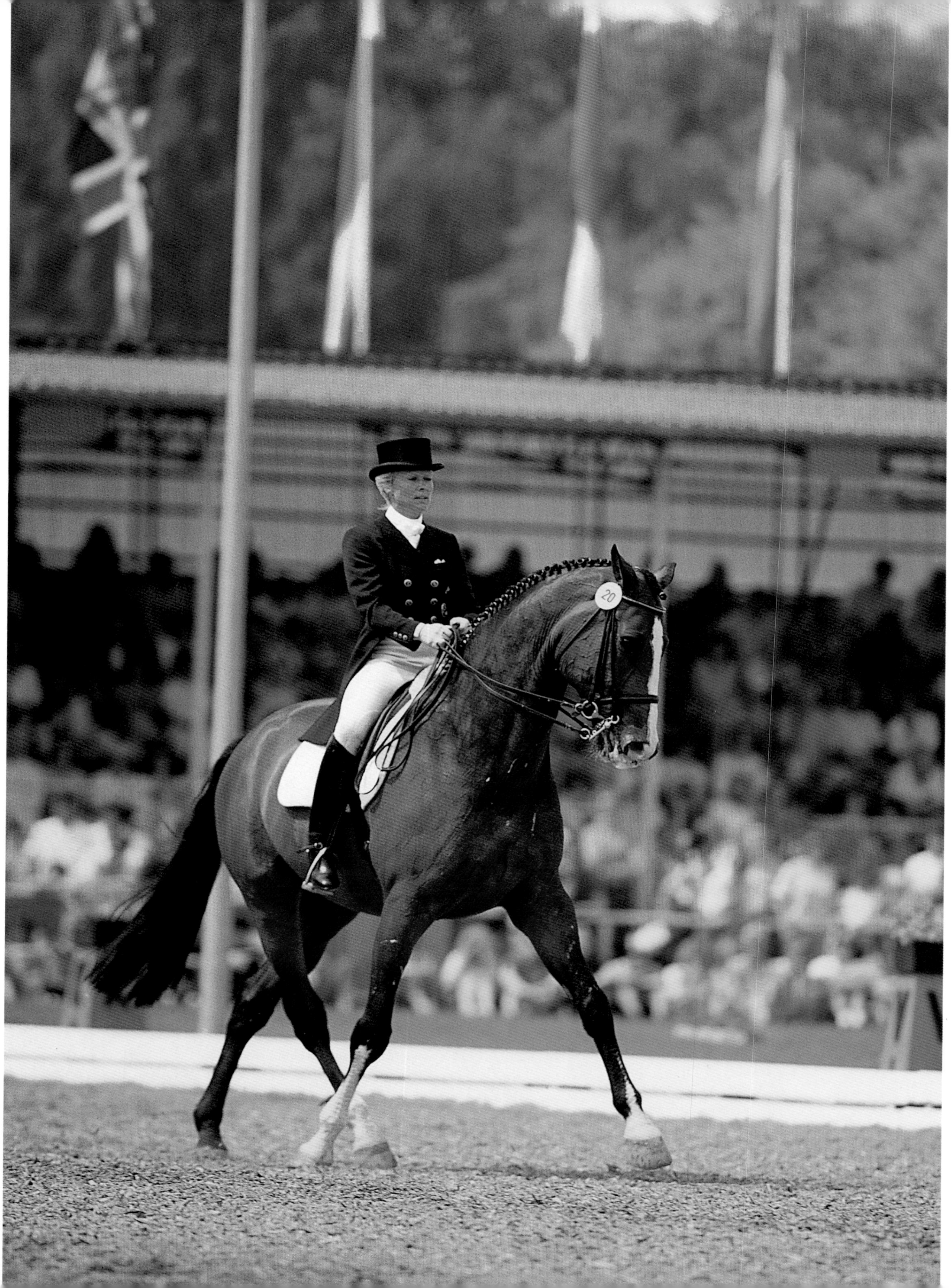
20

Although Margit Otto-Crépin was born in Germany, since her marriage to a Frenchman she has always ridden for France. Margit first hit the headlines in dressage when riding the wonderfully elegant gelding, Corlandus. Together they became the 1987 European Champions. The following year they went on to win an individual silver medal at the Seoul Olympics. In 1989 they won an individual silver medal at the European Championships, as well as winning the World Cup Final. At the 1991 European Championships they won the individual bronze medal. Margit retired Corlandus in 1995. Today, as a 23 year old, he enjoys being turned out and, to Margit's amazement, 'He is actually quite nice to the other horses. Something I never thought possible!'

Margit is a true amateur. She works hard in order to pursue her love of dressage and competition. She has never benefited from any form of sponsorship. Her job is in the fashion industry and she has her own designer collection in Paris, called Dane Couture. Margit believes that competing and running a fashion business have similarities. 'In fashion, you have to buy the material then design the garment. Later on you take your collection to the fashion show where you show off your creation. The clients either buy your garments or they don't. It's like buying a young horse, which is your material. Then you train the horse, put all the work into it, like designing and sewing. Then you compete and show off what you have worked on. In competition you don't receive orders from clients but you get marks from the judges that tell you very clearly whether you've done a good job or not.

'As for Corlandus, he has an exceptional personality! He was super in his extensions as well as in his collected work but horribly difficult to ride!'

Asked whether she still thinks back on tests that might not have been as faultless as she would have wished, Margit is quick to point out that she never lives in the past! 'The test I rode one hour ago is already out of my mind and I think about the next one. This attitude is also related to my work. Every year has to be different. You have to create something new. If you live in the past, your new collection won't look any different and you simply won't succeed. The same applies to the test you ride. The horse reacts differently every time. You can never say that you'd like to ride the test the same way as you rode it two weeks ago. One day I could ride a test almost faultlessly. The next day my horse might do things he has never done before. It happens! I think that a rider has to be totally aware and awake at all times!'

German rider Karin Rehbein and the fifteen-year-old Oldenburger stallion Donnerhall accomplished one of their greatest achievements at the 1997 European Championships by being placed third individually as well as winning a team gold medal. Although the pair had already won a team gold and an individual silver medal at the 1994 World Equestrian Games, Karin believes that their successes at Verden mean more to her. Sadly, Karin's husband and trainer, Herbert Rehbein, had died only a few months prior to the championships.

'Emotionally, the build up to Verden was very confusing for me. However, I was determined to do well because I knew how much Donnerhall was on form. I was very pleased with his performance. This picture was taken during the canter half pass, a movement that he has learned to master very well over the years. I must admit that it was usually me who had a problem with it! The counting used to confuse me terribly!

'Winning the individual bronze medal this time round meant a lot to me because we all had to ride all three disciplines. The outcome is therefore very fair. At first I thought that riding three tests might be too demanding for the horses but now I believe that it causes no problems to a well-trained horse. It was very hot in Verden and all the horses coped well. Putting a Kür together is a lot of work. I haven't really made huge changes in Donnerhall's freestyle programme over the years. I don't think that anybody has actually noticed! Dressage is like a drug! Training a young horse and noticing the improvements makes me so very happy!'

Donnerhall stands his ground in the world's most famous arenas, and also covers mares regularly. Karin describes his character as marvellous. 'He is so gentle and lovable. He is a real fighter at the show and will always give his best. He is radiant and knows it! The bigger the crowd, the better he will perform. His strength is his expression. Donnerhall has such a great presence. His piaffe, passage, canter pirouette and extended trot are superb. Donnerhall is truly my darling, always has been and always will be! Riding him gives me the most wonderful feeling!'

Dutch competitor Ellen Bontje is based in Germany where she works as a trainer and rider. She was a member of the silver-medal-winning team at the 1992 Barcelona Olympics when riding Larius.

In this picture Ellen is on the Holstein stallion, Silvano. They are on an extended canter across the diagonal at the 1997 European Championships where the Dutch team took the silver medal behind the Germans but ahead of the Swedish team.

Ellen has been riding Silvano since he was nine years old. She recalls that the first nine months were spent reschooling Silvano to her training method and that his weakest point at that time was his flying changes. After a great season in 1995, they were members of the silver-medal-winning team at the European Championships in Mondorf. Sadly, Silvano sustained a leg injury the same winter which meant that they missed out on competing at the Atlanta Olympics.

'Like most stallions, Silvano can be quite naughty! He has a lot of temperament and can be quite a handful at times. He can still get a bit overexcited at shows. His sensitivity can lead to some difficulties because he tends to overreact to my leg. However, Silvano is very expressive and I believe that one needs a horse with a lot of temperament to perform a good dressage test. I wasn't really happy with my Grand Prix in Verden. In fact, I was quite angry with myself, especially after seeing the marks we got. Although I knew we didn't do great, I couldn't believe that we were as bad as the marks made it look. I was still in a foul mood the following day! However, that changed after the Special because I had made a much better job of it! I do usually get a little nervous a few hours before my test but as soon as I start warming up my nervousness disappears because I am with my horse and feel comfortable. But let me give you a tip. It wouldn't be wise to come and ask me for an interview two hours before my test! I do need time to concentrate mentally!'

British rider Annie McDonald-Hall remembers thinking that German-bred Floriani was fantastic the day she set eyes on him. She tried him out in Germany and then brought him back to Great Britain. At the time Annie was looking for a Grand Prix horse and knew that Floriani and his former rider, Herbert Krug, had been members of the German team who won the 1987 European gold medal at Goodwood. As Annie explains, it took a while before she really got to know Floriani well. They formed a great partnership but, sadly, Floriani died just before the 1992 Barcelona Olympics. Now Annie has a string of promising young horses and hopes to be competing at top level soon. Here Floriani and Annie are pictured while warming up for the 1990 Grand Prix at Goodwood.

'Although Floriani was an experienced horse when I got him, he was very sensitive but also a bit lazy with it. So there were two sides to him and you really had to hit it right! He was a lovely horse with a fun character. He had a temperament more like a dog than a horse. In Germany he was just treated like a horse so he was not particularly fond of humans and it took a while before he became a household pet, which is what he was with me.

'I thought he was great the minute I saw him. However, it took me a while before I got used to him. He was pretty determined and it took me some time to get flying changes on him. Piaffe and passage were what he loved doing. He could also do a canter pirouette on a sixpence but changes were difficult. I used to get into a right tiz about them! It would go from bad to worse but I got them in the end.

'Floriani was an extremely beautiful horse. When I first walked into his stable, there stood this black, gleaming creature, and I knew that he could produce really good work. If he was a human, I guess he would probably have been the black sheep of the family – naughty but fun!'

Irish rider Anna Merveldt recalls always having been horse mad! While eventing in Ireland she recognised that dressage was somewhat her weak point and decided some fifteen years ago to travel to Germany to improve it. Anna trained for five years with Prince Auersberg, a man who might not be very well known outside Germany but who rides and teaches the classical principles. Anna then met and married a German vet and has made Germany her home. She has never looked back to her eventing days. 'After being in Germany and seeing how dressage can be ridden and realising how horses can go, I just knew that I would have to stick with dressage!'

She has since represented Ireland at all major international shows, including the Olympic Games and various championships. Here she is pictured at the 1997 European Championships, riding fourteen-year-old Belgian-bred Rousseau. Anna bought Rousseau as a ten year old and brought him up to Grand Prix level. Later, having received an offer for Rousseau that she could hardly refuse, Anna decided to sell him. 'I was a little disappointed with our performance at Verden because Rousseau didn't really go nicely there. He had been going so well in the build up to the European and can go so much better than he did. He was definitely too excited there!

'Rousseau was a very sensitive horse who was always willing to work. He had a super mind for dressage. Maybe a little bit too hot at times but I could live with that! I remember the first time I saw his face and eye just thinking, "That's him!". He was a real fighter in the good sense. Very intelligent and extremely amusing. A fantastic horse. I loved him dearly!'

American rider Carol Lavell and her
gelding, Gifted, travelled to Goodwood
in 1992 as part of their build up for the
Barcelona Olympics. Carol bought Gifted
as an unbroken four year old in 1984 in
Germany and, thanks to her relentless
dedication and hard work, slowly took him
to Grand Prix level. Unfortunately, Gifted
died from a mysterious disease in January
1997. Carol has hugely fond memories of
him as well as of Goodwood, not only
because Gifted won the Grand Prix there
but because Goodwood is her 'absolutely
favourite show in the whole world!'. Here
they are pictured during the warm up,
putting the finishing touches to the piaffe
before entering the arena.

'Gifted learned the piaffe very easily.
It only took one lesson of just walking
beside him. However, he always had great
difficulties with the piaffe because he was
so big that he found it hard to lift himself
up to do the job properly. He couldn't get
his hindquarters low enough and therefore
didn't have enough expression with it. As
he got physically stronger he started to
perform it much better. I assume that he
didn't really like the movement very much
but he never displayed any resistance.

'Gifted was difficult in as much as he
was a very sensitive horse. He was very
territorial and liked his stall to himself.
He didn't want any other horses around
bothering him. The same applied to people.
He didn't like them to come and stare at
him. If he wanted to see people it was on
his own terms!

'Gifted had an enormous heart! He
could put together a fantastic test.
However, lots of times he could only get
one test done and then the next time
things were not so good for him although
he tried. Because he was so big he had to
put everything into one really good
performance and then maybe the next test
wouldn't be near as good even though his
heart was in it.'

Carol Lavell and her German-bred Gifted were members of the US team who won the bronze medal at the 1992 Barcelona Olympics. Carol sees their achievement as a bit of a miracle because the entire team had a stroke of bad luck only a fortnight before the games when all their horses contracted a virus. The horses were laid off with high temperatures and by the time they arrived in Barcelona they were a touch short of training! Here Carol and Gifted are performing an extended canter across the diagonal. Asked about the feeling Gifted gave her during the test, Carol admits that, sadly, she has hardly any recollections of it!

'If I had one wish in my whole life, I'd like to go back now and ride my test over so that I could remember what it was really like! There was just so much pressure and so many things going wrong on the way to the Olympics that it all seems rather clouded. I look at the press cuttings and wonder what it must have felt like!

'As for the extended canter, it was the most difficult speed for Gifted. I remember German trainer Herbert Rehbein telling me that he thought Gifted would never learn to canter! What you see here took years of hard work. Further, I remember a judge taking me aside after my test during the North American Dressage Championships to tell me what the extended canter should look like. "His neck and nose have to go out and he has to reach for his canter." I could only reply: "Boy, I would really love that to happen!" I really tried hard the next day in the Special and won both the individual and team gold medal! It was the first time a judge had taken me aside to tell me what I needed to do. I was so happy that a judge would show such concern about the development of a horse! Of course it doesn't happen overnight but, boy, did I try hard to express that in the canter the next day!

'What I liked most about Gifted are all the things I miss now and I regret not having! Every day the ride was wonderful. Every day I rode him made my day! He was huge and yet so light and graceful. He was able to display enormous power without pulling on the reins and without losing his self-carriage. He had a lot of personality. He was so sensitive that if one made too strong a demand on him, one would lose everything.'

British rider Jane Bredin formed a great partnership with the Dutch-bred gelding Cupido from the moment his owner, Susie Cumine, asked Jane to take over because he had become a touch too strong for her. Jane regularly takes Cupido to Holland where she trains with Sjef Janssen. In their first Grand Prix season they were selected to compete at the 1994 World Equestrian Games where they were placed eleventh in the Kür. Jane reckons that their best achievement to date was coming third with the team at the 1995 CDIO in Aachen, as well as winning both the Grand Prix and the Special at Hickstead the same year. Cupido has had his fair share of bad luck due to past injuries. Here they are pictured during the Grand Prix at the 1997 CDIO in Hickstead.

'Riding at Hickstead in 1997 was probably bad timing in as much as I knew I had to get him out to a new show after his lay off. Cupido wasn't on any current form because he had had so much time off since his sickness in Atlanta. Competing with him was just a necessary process to prove to people that he was still

around and that he would be back at the top. I had a bad ride in terms of not feeling confident about his form and the good bits he did were not necessarily seen positively by the judges because they hadn't seen Cupido for a long time. It's a shame because, all in all, Cupido has been off with injury or sickness for eighteen months in the last two and a half years.

'As for his personality, he is a head case! A total extrovert! He is very much a VIP and he knows it. He is very strong physically as well as mentally. He likes his game and knows that he can do the job. He is very confident in the arena. He is a real show off. He can also be a bit of a bully. He used to sail across the diagonal and have a buck. The first international we did at Addington, he was just a bit overexcited in the piaffe and suddenly he bucked and landed in front of the judge's box. He wasn't being naughty, he was just overexcited. However it was pretty dramatic. I just stopped and proceeded in piaffe where we had landed! By no means is he malicious. It is just a form of expression. Now the piaffe has become one of his strongest points, together with the passage. He is always enthusiastic about his work. It might sound a bit corny but I have been known to say that if he was human I'd marry him!'

Susie Cumine has owned Cupido since he was five and rode him when he was a baby. In September 1993 Susie asked Jane to take Cupido on to Grand Prix level. By February of the following year Jane and Cupido were longlisted for the 1994 World Equestrian Games in The Hague.

'Getting to the World Championship was just brilliant. It was my first big show as an owner and the atmosphere was just exceptional. As an owner you were just so much part of the horse. There I was allowed to be with my horse as opposed to the Olympics in Atlanta where owners were kept away from their horse and their rider a lot more. In The Hague I felt so much more part of it. Watching a test is, however, quite stressful! You feel as if you are actually riding the test yourself! I know what Jane is supposed to be doing and I just hope that it's happening. It's like I'm holding my breath all the way through the test although I know that there is absolutely nothing I can do. In a way it's a relief when the test is over because mentally I am with Jane all the time. I know that Jane is trying her hardest and that Cupido can do it. So I just hope that they gel together. You get to relax a bit once the test is over but then you have to wait for the scores! I quite often wish the scores didn't have to come! I always have to remember all the movements they have done exactly because when Jane comes out she always asks me what the test was like.'

German rider Monica Theodorescu is the daughter
of well-known trainer George Theodorescu who left
Romania some 40 years ago to settle in Germany.
Monica was born in Germany and started to ride
a pony under her father's guidance at the age of
three. Monica has never ridden with anybody but
her father and points out that they form an
excellent team. In this picture, taken during the
1996 CDIO at Aachen, she is performing a canter
pirouette with the fifteen-year-old Hanoverian
gelding Grunox. Aachen is not only one of the most
famous shows worldwide, it is also the most
important show for the Germans because, depending
on the year, it is always used as a selection trial for
the European or World Championships or the
Olympic Games.

'Other than riding at championships, Aachen is
the most difficult show for us Germans! We ride
under a lot of pressure there because every one of
us wants to make the team. Grunox performed very
well that year and we went on to win the team gold
medal at the Atlanta Olympics.

'As for the pirouette, it is one of Grunox's best
movements. He learned it really fast and it has
always been a highlight in his test. He has rarely
made a mistake in the pirouette and we always
received high marks for them. I was really pleased
with his form all through 1996. He had another
brilliant season in 1997, winning with the team in
Aachen as well as winning the Hamburg Derby and
Wiesbaden. Grunox is in retirement now but I still
ride him daily. We truly had a superb partnership!'

German rider Monica Theodorescu has an impressive record of achievements. In the late eighties and early nineties, when partnered with the black gelding Ganimedes, she won a team gold medal at the Seoul Olympics, a team gold medal at the 1989 European Championships and a team gold and an individual bronze medal at the 1990 World Equestrian Games. In 1993 and 1994, still riding Ganimedes, Monica won two consecutive World Cup finals.

Her list of successes with Grunox is just as formidable. Together they won a team gold and the individual silver medal at the 1993 European Championships. They also won a team gold medal at the 1992 Barcelona Olympics, an achievement they repeated four years later in Atlanta. In this picture Monica is riding Grunox in extended trot during the Grand Prix at the Barcelona Olympics.

'The most difficult part of the day was dealing with the heat! We recorded forty-four degrees centigrade in the shade! It was really tricky to handle Grunox's energies efficiently. He went extremely well, especially in his extensions. He really could trot!

'He wasn't the easiest of horses as a youngster. He would get frightened at times and suddenly run off! However, Grunox soon turned out to be a very reliable partner and we had a very special relationship. I wouldn't say that he was special to me solely because of our achievements. His character played a big role too. Without the right character, a horse will never take you to those type of heights. We spent a lot of time together and the good results are purely the reward for the work we had put into it. It's like the icing on the cake!'

British rider Emile Faurie has clocked up his greatest achievements to date with the bay gelding Virtu. The pair became British National Champions in 1993 and 1994. During the 1993 European Championships they won a team silver as well as an individual bronze medal in the Special. Virtu took Emile to the Barcelona Olympics which was an all-time dream for Emile. They were also placed fourth individually at the 1994 World Equestrian Games.

Emile decided to retire Virtu, at the age of sixteen, in the autumn of 1994, but still hacks him out regularly around the fields at his Gloucestershire establishment. 'I can cry just thinking about Virtu! He is such an amazing horse. To understand you would need to have seen him when he first came to me. He was such a fat lazy lump and he was uninspiring to watch. However, he developed such an incredible character because, for the first time in his life, he knew that people loved him! Love is always the making of a great horse. Nicole worships Rembrandt. Anky worships the ground Bonfire walks on. I love Virtu so much because he was an underdog when he started off. This might be romantic but I am always on the side of the victim. However, I do believe that if a horse is made to feel important it will perform better and give its all! To begin with Virtu was a total introvert but he ended up being an outright extrovert. He learned to love life and he was totally at ease with his own body. Over the years he became more and more extrovert, exuberant, soft and athletic.

'Winning the individual bronze medal with Virtu was like having all my Christmasses at once! I also had a great feeling on him at the 1994 World Equestrian Games. I knew that he was ready. We came fourth and in a way I think he was cheated. I watched the test over and over again and I know that he was better. He gave me a great ride. He was fourth and that's cool by me.

'Virtu really was a lot of fun to ride. I know that he likes me too because I don't think any horse could have given what he gave me at the European if they didn't like their rider! Similarly if you are not passionate about the horse you are riding, you shouldn't ride it! For me Virtu is the epitome of what dressage should be: harmony, grace and expression.'

Nadine Capellmann-Biffar's biggest win to date was a gold medal with the German team at the 1997 European Championships held in Verden, Germany.

Nadine was born into a horse-loving family. Her father used to show jump as well as compete in dressage and she started to ride at the age of four. In Verden she rode twelve-year-old Gracioso, a horse she acquired from her trainer, Klaus Balkenhol, in 1995. Nadine bought Gracioso during his first year at Grand Prix level. The pair hit it off from the very start and were placed second in a Grand Prix only ten days after they became partners.

In this picture Nadine and Gracioso are doing one-time flying changes during the European Championships. 'Gracioso is a very kind horse with a strong personality. He only needs subtle aids and those have to be finely tuned. In actual fact I only have to think about the movement I want him to do and he will do it! He is rather nervous and can get pretty hot at times. At a show I generally have to get him used to the surroundings first before he calms down. I was really happy winning with the team although I must admit that I was slightly disappointed to have missed the individual bronze medal by such a narrow margin. But don't get me wrong, the hours after the prizegiving for the team event were the happiest of my life. Winning was fantastic. It represents all I have worked for over the years! Gracioso is definitely the best horse I have ever owned. His strongest characteristic must be his sensitivity! None the less, we do share a perfect understanding of one another! I truly hope that we will be in the team for the Sydney Olympics!'

British rider Carl Hester and the German-bred stallion Giorgione both made their international debut at Grand Prix level in the spring of 1992 when competing in Hertogenbosch where they were placed fifth. Later that year, Carl and Giorgione came third at Goodwood and fifth at the prestigious Wiesbaden Show in Germany. Once they had won all the British selection trials, Carl, only 23 at the time, and Giorgione were well on their way to representing Great Britain at the 1992 Barcelona Olympics.

Here they are, sailing across the diagonal in extended trot during one of the hottest afternoons in Barcelona. 'I remember thinking I might pass out because it was so hot! Giorgione was also quite affected by the heat but I knew that the one thing he was going to show during his test was his extended trot. And he did! Giorgione was probably the horse of my lifetime! The extended trot was his speciality. It was what he was known for and what I loved riding the most with him.

He was a marvellous horse! He helped me to make a name for myself and gave me the first proper feeling of a very powerful Grand Prix horse! As a stallion he has a remarkable personality. He is very kind, very gentle but highly powerful to ride.

'Taking part at the Olympics was a tremendous feeling. The one thing that struck me more than anything was the opening ceremony. Walking into the Olympic stadium with thousands of people looking on created an incredible atmosphere! It made me feel weak and wobbly, wondering if I'd ever spot a face I knew? During the competition itself I felt safe because we are all friends. However, the other thing that made it very special for me was when riding around the edge of the arena, I suddenly heard my father's voice coming from the stands and shouting! "Go for it, Carl!". I hadn't seen my father for over a year and didn't know that he was there.

'As for my best achievement with Giorgione, it must be winning the National Championship that same year. I think that test was the best Grand Prix I have ridden to date! Giorgione is majestic. He is great looking and has fabulous movements. He has everything you could ever hope for in a dressage horse!'

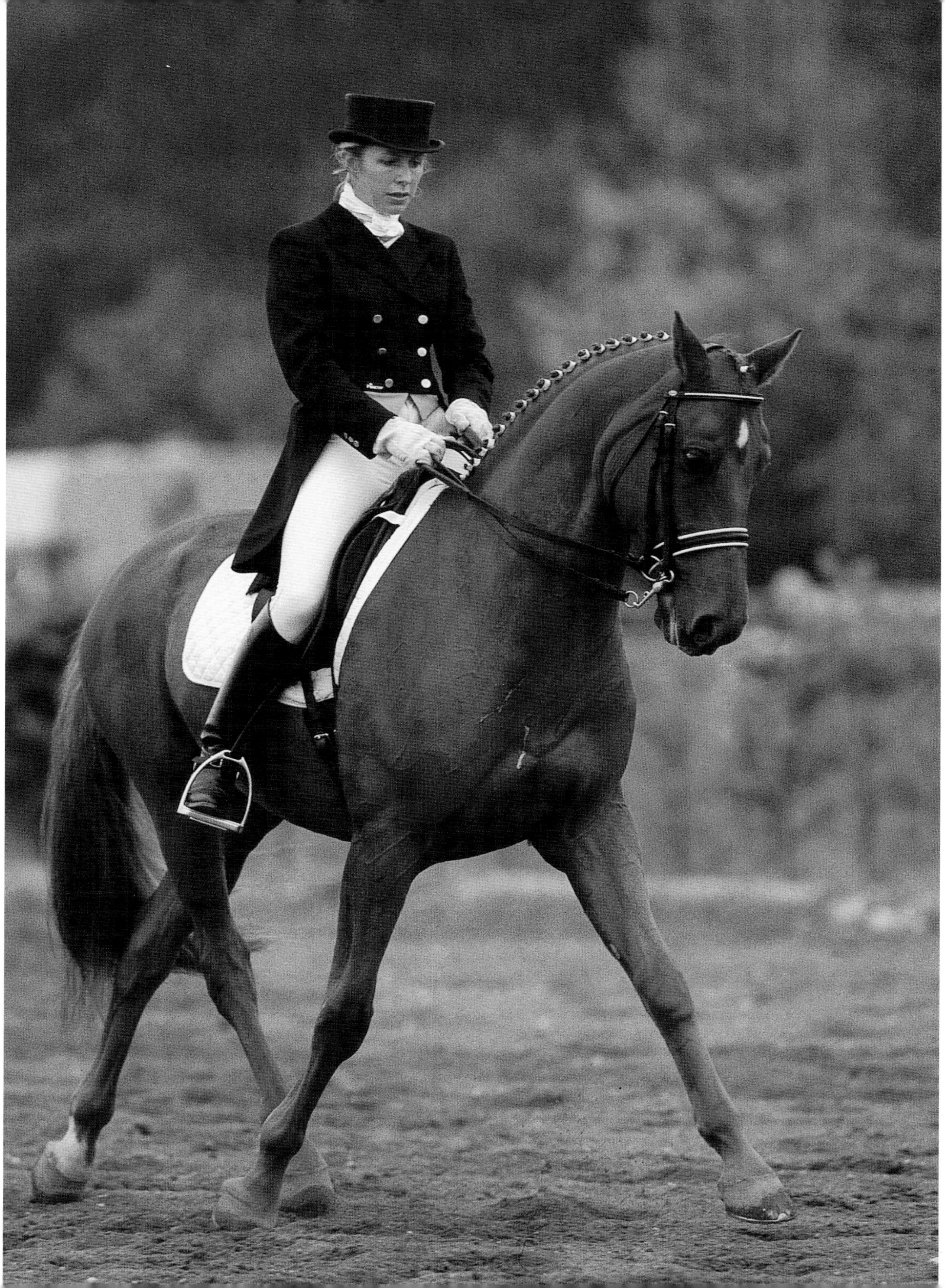

British rider Vicky Thompson made a name for herself in top-level dressage competition when partnered with the Dutch-bred chestnut gelding, Enfant. In 1996 they were chosen to represent Great Britain with the team at the CDIO in Aachen. The two helped the British Team into second place behind the Germans. The same year the pair were also members of the British Team at the Atlanta Olympics. Shortly after, Enfant's owner, Elaine Smith, decided to have him back for her own use.

Vicky started her career in showing and first began to work with Austrian-born trainer Franz Rochowansky fifteen years ago. Here Vicky and Enfant are pictured during the 1994 National Championships at Addington.

'The half pass wasn't one of our easier movements! However, Enfant has a lot of energy and ability. He is also very elastic but yet difficult to keep exactly in his rhythm. I also found it difficult to keep his neck in the correct position. He was quite easy to understand and we soon formed a good relationship. Enfant is supremely intelligent and very sharp. He is a horse that is always ready to work underneath you. I never had to ask him to engage more. He usually offered more than he should offer. I had to sit very carefully on him. I had to keep my hands forward and let him stretch out into the bridle at all times. I had to ride him completely off my seat and legs. He used to pick up on atmosphere very easily and it was interesting to see how he usually picked himself up even more when we entered the arena.'

German rider Ulla Salzgeber and the strikingly elegant chestnut
gelding Rusty had a fair bit of luck on the way to winning a
team gold medal at the 1997 European Championships. Early
in 1997 Ulla qualified nine-year-old Rusty for the small
competition at the CDIO in Aachen. However, because Reiner
Klimke couldn't compete in the big competition, the pair
were allowed to take his spot and ride as individuals. Rusty
went exceptionally well in the Grand Prix and in the Special
and the pair were fifth-best Germans on both accounts.
Although the selectors had their reservations because of
Rusty's young age, he was still put on the long list for the
forthcoming championships.

Their other selection trials were at the National
Championships. There, Ulla and Rusty had a bad day which Ulla
puts down to being nervous. After that unfortunate experience,
Ulla rode at another small show in her home state of Bavaria and
decided to give Rusty a rest. A week before the championships,
Ulla was sitting on Rusty ready to take him out for a hack
when she received a phone call from the selectors asking her
whether Rusty was fit because 'He's in the team!' Both Monica
Theodorescu's and Martin Schaudt's horses had problems and so
it was up to Rusty and Ulla to bail them out! Ulla, the Young
Riders' European Champion of 1977, rose to the occasion.

'Although I had only three days of training, I was delighted
because I could finally show everybody what Rusty and I were
made of! At the time I had only ridden Rusty for just over two
years but I knew what a great horse he is. Rusty's first international appearance was in Aachen and I was thrilled with his
placing, especially as he was a newcomer as far as the judges
were concerned. At Verden, Rusty showed some weakness in the
walk and in the piaffe. However, a few months down the road
he had already hugely improved his piaffe. All other movements
are true highlights. He has already scored tens for his extensions
and half passes. In the canter pirouette he scores eights and I'd
like to improve that by a mark or two!

'Rusty is such a talented horse. He loves to work and learns
very fast. If he has a little problem with a movement, such as
the piaffe, you only have to give him time and then suddenly it
clicks which is what's happened over the winter months. Now
he really enjoys the piaffe!

'Rusty has a very strong personality. Let's put it this way,
he doesn't like doing it with everybody! He is quite selective!
I am the only one who rides him. I know his every move and
his moods and I know in advance when he is about to wiggle
his ear! I don't think that one could find another Rusty in the
whole wide world. Currently, I wouldn't know of a better
dressage horse!'

US rider Michelle Gibson found herself in the role of local hero during the 1996 Atlanta Olympics, a part she played exceedingly well by scoring the highest marks in the American squad and thereby helping the US team to a bronze medal. Sadly, Michelle sat on Peron for the last time while competing in the freestyle because Peron's owners decided to send their stallion back to Germany after the games. Knowing between 40 to 50 people in the crowd made Michelle slightly nervous but she appreciated the support her family and friends gave her just by their presence. Michelle felt under pressure because she wanted to do well, especially for her parents' sake. 'My family have supported me in every possible way. They have done without so that I could be in Germany and learn to ride!'

Michelle first travelled to Rudolf Zeilinger's yard in 1989 to further her interest in dressage. After an article about Michelle was printed in a 1993 edition of the Atlanta *Journal*, Peron's owner called Michelle to show her a very overweight and out of shape horse. 'I went to see Peron, tried him out and took him home two weeks later! I had ridden lots of horses by that time but I wasn't really experienced in picking out horses. Although Peron had been out in the field for two months, he did everything I asked him for. Whether he could do it or not, he really tried for me. This is what I liked so much about him. He just had a big heart and I thought I'd give it a go. However, Peron was quite confused. I would ask him for one-time flying changes and he'd give me one line one time and none the next with the exact same aids.

'Because I didn't have enough experience to bring a horse to Grand Prix level, I took Peron to Germany which was only possible thanks to the generous support of a number of people. Winning the bronze with the team was fantastic because the US scored the highest an American team ever scored at the Olympics and Peron did his fair share to pull the team through! I wish that we could have done better in the individual but I can't let this cloud the fact that we did a fabulous job.

'Peron is very much a one-person horse. He likes to have his time alone but he also likes to have some attention. He loves the crowd. Most horses have their funny little habits. Peron never did anything like drink Coca-Cola out of a bottle but he used to rest his head on my back when I put my spurs on! Peron will always be special to me for all we have been through and for being my first Olympic horse. I can't say that he is the horse of my lifetime. It could be that he is. However, I'd like to think that I'm going to have another pretty special horse some day!'

German rider Martin Schaudt and his fourteen-year-old horse Durgo first hit the international headlines in 1994 when they won their first Grand Prix in Donaueschingen, beating no less a pair than Klaus Balkenhol and Goldstern. Ever since, they have been watched very closely by the German selectors. After further consistent results, Martin and Durgo made it into the German team for the 1997 Atlanta Olympics. However, as Martin recalls, it hasn't always been plain sailing with Durgo and now that they have made it, the pressure continually to perform well is truly on.

'I bought Durgo as a five year old knowing that he was a difficult horse. The day I tried him he wouldn't stop rearing. However, I recognised that he had good qualities and never thought I wouldn't be able to get him right. Nevertheless, during the first six months absolutely nothing worked! Whenever I asked for something he would rear. I was close to giving up and thought if only I could have my money back! Knowing full well that nobody would ever buy him, however, I persevered. Finally, I adjusted to his ways and gradually saw us progressing. But it took a year before I could ride him normally.

'Durgo is a very strong horse. Even to this day when he senses that I want something he becomes defensive. He is dreadful to look after. He still bites and kicks. All in all, we do get along now but he is not the type of horse that would give you anything freely. His strengths are surely his piaffe and passage. We always get good marks for them. However, the feeling I get on him has never corresponded to my ideals. The passage is truly fantastic though. He has such power which allows him to really push himself off the ground and float in the passage. If Durgo was human I am sure he would be a skinhead. When I give him an apple, he's not really grateful. He will bite because he believes that there has to be more where this one came from.'

German rider Martin Schaudt was truly grateful for the support he received from the crowds after his Grand Prix test at the 1997 Atlanta Olympics. 'I never felt more relieved after a test than after the Grand Prix in Atlanta! I had been under enormous pressure during the build up to the games. While training and during the warm up Durgo felt very lazy and lethargic. I therefore didn't know how he would perform in the test. When we finally got the test behind us I felt elated! I was so happy to notice banners with Durgo's name on them in the crowd. I draw a lot from such support!'

A Lusitano's hind legs in
ballet pose.

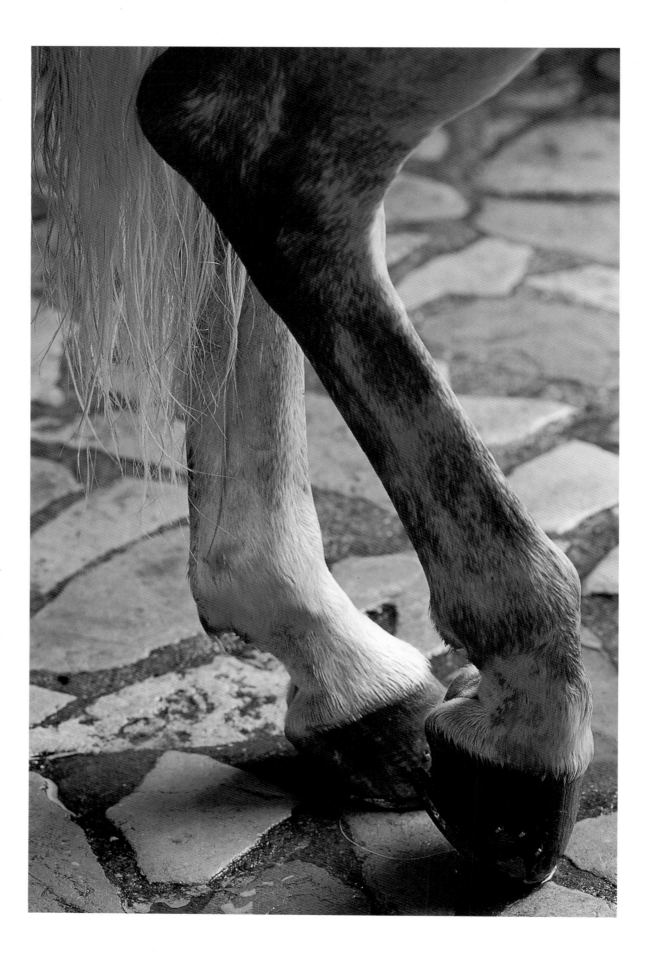

DRESSAGE TO MUSIC

Ever since the introduction of the Volvo World Cup for Show Jumping in 1978 and its consequent success, the supporters of dressage spoke of having a similar World Cup series in their own discipline. Dressage enthusiasts saw the creation of a new format as the perfect opportunity to revolutionise the sport by introducing a new element to it. Adding music to an already very artistic sport seemed to be the ideal answer if the goal of reaching a wider audience, as well as attracting serious sponsors, was going to be met. The principle of being able to choreograph one's own sequence of movements, all at Grand Prix level, to a personal choice of music, meant that a fresh dimension was undoubtedly going to appear.

After endless meetings and discussions in search of a suitable format that would incorporate the element of music, the World Cup for Dressage finally became a reality in 1985. The World Cup is based on the Kür to Music but has the Grand Prix serving as qualification for the Kür.

The inception of the World Cup series meant that first preliminary events were held between May 1985 and March 1986 with the inaugural World Cup Final taking place in the Brabant Hallen of Hertogenbosch in the Netherlands between March 21–23 1986. Anne-Grethe Jensen of Denmark, on Marzog, emerged as the first World Cup Champion, winning both the

Grand Prix and the Kür to Music. The pair's excellent performance and the high level of entertainment it gave, helped to set the standard for a fixture that was here to stay.

A few years later, the championships followed suit. The 1991 European Dressage Championships saw the introduction of two separate individual medals. One was given for the traditional Grand Prix Special and one for the Kür to Music. Sven Rothenberger, still competing for Germany at the time, won the Kür and, therefore, one of the European titles on Andiamo.

The 1993 European Championships held in Lipica adopted the same format. This time the Kür title went to Nicole Uphoff-Becker, riding Grand Gilbert. Laura Fry and Quarryman just missed out on a medal and were placed fourth, a mere 0.7 points behind the Hungarian Gyula Dallos and Aktion.

Now it was time for the 1994 World Equestrian Games, held in The Hague, also to award separate medals to those riders who could produce the best presentations to music. The standard of the competition was both highly colourful and stimulating. German rider Klaus Balkenhol and Goldstern produced an exquisite interpretation to a Spanish theme that will remain in people's minds for a long time to come. However, his performance was slightly overshadowed by the equally memorable performance of Dutch

rider Anky van Grunsven and the flamboyant gelding Bonfire. This pair brought a further dimension to the competition by performing to a specially arranged piece of music. The combination of Anky's choreography of perfectly executed movements, together with the music, caught the imagination of both judges and spectators alike.

Anky's excellence and innovative effort paid off. The pair were crowned World Champions in the Kür to Music.

For the 1996 Atlanta Olympics a new format was adopted and only one set of medals was given for individual merit. The climax of the competition and the concluding decision as to who was to become Olympic Champion depended very much on the final leg, the Kür to Music, also referred to as the freestyle. From the 25 riders who qualified for the Grand Prix Special, thirteen went on to the freestyle in a quest for the Olympic title. The total sum of points acquired from the Grand Prix, the Grand Prix Special and the freestyle confirmed the winner. The new arrangement proved very popular. However, it now means that every rider has to consider putting together a Kür, whereas, before, riders could still choose which path to take.

The marks for the freestyle are divided into two categories. The first set of marks is given for the technical execution of the movements. The second set comprises artistic marks. These are subdivided into marks for rhythm, energy and elasticity; marks for harmony between rider and horse; marks for choreography, use of arena and inventiveness; marks for the degree of difficulty and well-calculated risks;

and, finally, marks for choice of music and the interpretation of it.

By talking to various riders it became clear to me that not every horse is suitable for the Kür. Nicole Uphoff-Becker didn't like taking Rembrandt into a Kür because he could spook or sidestep, which meant that their movements could, at times, be a fraction behind the music which defeated the objective of a harmonious picture. Grand Gilbert, on the other hand, seemed perfect for the job and won Nicole a European gold medal in 1993.

However, now that the freestyle is an established feature in the make up of all championships, every top rider needs to train his or her horse accordingly. Riders need to put a lot of work into choreographing their programme and into choosing suitable music for it.

My personal reflection on the Kür is that it gives riders a marvellous opportunity to show off their creativity and ingenuity. However, when it comes to their choice of music, I must admit that I am frequently disappointed in the quality and type of music that riders choose. Most riders simply ride to a few cut-together pieces of popular themes, believing that if the pieces of music are well known, preferably liked by the public and 'sort of fit' trot or canter, then the performance will be well received. My view is that these riders are missing the point. They are far from exhausting the limitless potential for making a real mark. Not only does music reach one of our most developed senses and bring us tremendous pleasure, it is also a wonderful tool that goes hand in hand with movement. The effect of combining movement and music is already well demonstrated in ballet and dance in general. Comparing the Kür to ballet is not too farfetched. The elegance and skills of the dressage movements are forms of expression and can only be enhanced by the right choice of music. Similarly to ballet, a Kür can also tell an imaginary story.

Anky van Grunsven is one of only a few riders to have the right idea. She rides to uninterrupted, specially composed pieces of music that have quality and will allow the spectators' imaginations to flow while they also enjoy the visually harmonious performance.

Emile Faurie also chose to have a piece of music specially composed for Mary Madha's horse, Legrini. In the following pages Emile shares his views on what dressage to music means to him. I also spoke to Neil Douek and Lara Greenway, the composers of the piece 'Pour L'âme de Legrini', specially written for Emile's Kür.

Emile Faurie

'The value of dressage to music is obvious. It puts bums on seats. But it's like everything else in life. If it's done well, it's magnificent to watch. Done badly, it's absolutely ghastly to watch!'

Emile Faurie used to be the worse critic when dressage to music was first created and thought of it as circus rubbish. 'Now I believe that it is fantastic and, most important, we have to do it properly because it is the only way forward in our sport.

'If riders choose a piece of music and try to ride to it, they are doing it wrong. The music has to complement the horse and the horse has to complement the music. The chosen music has to create a mood. Riders who try to select music because of a nice beat or a pleasant rhythm are on a loser. A piece of music

British rider Emile Faurie used to be the severest critic of dressage to music. Now he thinks it's fantastic!

has to stir up emotions in the watching audience.

'A beat only works very occasionally. Klaus Balkenhol rode his Kür to a Spanish theme at the 1994 World Equestrian Games in The Hague. There it

Lara Greenway and Neil Douek are pictured in Neil's studio where 'Pour L'âme de Legrini', the piece of music for Emile's Kür, was composed. In creating Emile's Kür Neil and Lara moved into a relatively new area. 'We had nothing to compare our work with because all we had heard were cut-together pieces. However, we loved the challenge and we would do it again. Seeing a piece of music work is very gratifying. Composing is never the same. Creating the Kür for another horse would be a further wonderful challenge.'

worked superbly. It created a most fantastic atmosphere. But it's one in a million. The man is a genius!

'I believe that riders should choose music that tells a story and creates a feeling. When Nina Menkova came second on Dickson in the 1991 World Cup Final, she rode to a piece of Russian violin music. It sounded almost unreal and like a screaming cat but it was phenomenal and created such a magnificent mood.

'Some riders use music that the audience tap their feet to in the rhythm of the beat in the hope that it might influence the judges. But at championship level nothing should distract the judges from the technical aspect of what is going on in front of them.

'A wonderful piece of music will enrich the

performance. A mood will hopefully have been created and the horse and rider will simply perform to it. It is similar to a human dancing to music. When watching ballet we don't put the dancer in question by saying, "What use is he in the whole exercise?" No, we recognise that through the dance and with the music a story is being told. The music and the performer blend into one. The two become a complete and utter partnership. That is just the way it has to be in the Kür.

'Fortunately for the sport, dressage to music is here to stay. And the only thing we can do now is to make it as pure and as beautiful to watch as possible.'

The challenge of choreographing his own test as well as choosing the perfect music is exciting for Emile. 'When choreographing I like everything to be in squares, in balance and as symmetrical as possible. Almost like mirror images. I think that it makes it easier to watch for the judges as well as for the audience. People don't want to sit through a Kür having to think too much. They want to see something that makes sense. If your choreography is too difficult to follow, it makes people stand back. I therefore try to keep simple and clear lines, as opposed to erratic ones.'

Asked whether it is difficult to please judges as well as the audience when putting together a Kür, Emile points out that: 'Although it is very important to put creative thoughts into it, a good performance is always going to get good marks, regardless of the choreography. If the horse is technically one hundred per cent correct, the chances of winning are good.' Emile was also quick to add: 'Thank God, because this is the saviour of dressage! At the end of the day you have to produce the goods – an excellent piaffe where the horse is in absolute balance and rhythm, or straight flying changes, for example. The most important factor, regardless of the type of competition, is still to produce a horse that is soft, harmonious and elegant to watch. The choreography is important because of the whole picture you present and, yes, marks are given for it but it cannot be the be all and end all. Riders shouldn't get away with a lack in technical quality just because of good choreography.'

During a Kür, some riders perform movements such as the pirouette or flying change by putting their reins in one hand. This is scored under the marks given for the degree of difficulty and is looked upon more favourably. Emile, however, doesn't think that one should be awarded extra marks for this because: 'If a horse goes one hundred per cent correctly, one should be able to perform all the movements without any hands whatsoever. Besides, it is rather gimmicky. Do you then ride the entire test in one hand to win?'

When putting together a Kür, Emile believes that one has to have a methodical approach. 'Firstly, you have to immediately look at your horse's strong points. Once you know them you will make them your main feature and be sure to show them in the best possible way. This means positioning, let's say, your piaffe in the arena where all five judges are able to see it at its best. Further, you have to be careful never to face a judge in an uncompromising position. Never place a movement at an odd angle to the judges. I try to draft my choreography in a way that is easy on the judges'

eyes because I want the judges to concentrate on the execution of my movement so that they are willing to give me good marks, and not have them guessing where my lines will end.'

Once all the compulsory movements have been incorporated into the choreography, Emile will also end his Kür with an emphasis on his horse's strong points so that they stick in the judges' minds. He stresses, however, that it is important to keep things simple. 'The most successful things in life are the most simple one. The simpler something is, the easier it is to interpret and the more elegant it is going to be.'

Once the choreography has been established it is time to think about the music. Emile is clear in saying that the visual effect comes first and that the music is brought in to enhance it. 'My main question when choosing my music will always be to consider the sort of horse I am performing with. For Legrini, who is a light and elegant horse, I wanted very moody music which is perhaps not as rhythmical as it would be for a horse that is itself naturally very rhythmical. The choice of music depends on the build and make up of the horse.'

Emile believes in riding to music that has been specially composed for the Kür, as opposed to music that has been cobbled together from existing pieces. 'Specially composed music is much easier to watch. Not very many people like their senses to be disturbed. If you are in one mood you don't like that to be disturbed by a sudden change. A continuous piece enhances the horse's performance. The Kür should have a meaning.'

It is very clear to Emile that whenever he rides a Kür he wants to tell a story. Through Legrini's owner, Mary Madha, Emile got to know the composers Lara Greenway and Neil Douek who have written music together for some considerable time. Emile felt it was important to brief the composers on how he saw Legrini. 'I see him as a shy horse that eventually grows in confidence. A horse that almost enters the arena a little timid and then grows to eventually shine and become a star. I also wanted to create the same mood throughout the piece but wanted it to rise to some form of crescendo. It is important to visualise a beginning and an end. I asked Lara and Neil to adapt the music to give a beginning and an end as well. Like it is demonstrated in any great symphony really. They came up with a piece they entitled, "Pour L'âme de Legrini" (for the soul of Legrini) and it is absolutely fabulous.'

Emile stresses that the music has to be customised to suit the horse because he believes that riding to a piece that fits his horse actually improves his riding. 'Legrini's music certainly influences me as a rider because I love listening to it. I often wonder whether some of the riders actually like the music they are riding to? If they do, there can't be much hope!'

Lara Greenway and Neil Douek

Oh but there is! The solution appears in the shape of Lara Greenway and Neil Douek. Before composing 'Pour L'âme de Legrini', these two young artists (Lara is 26 and Neil is 27) had worked together on composing the music for a film and had also written the lyrics and the music as well as the script for a musical.

Lara is an actress, writer and singer. Independently, she has written many jazz and blues pieces. She sees her acting as a huge advantage when it comes to composing because it has given her knowledge of movement in accordance with emotions.

During his studies at Middlesex University, Neil learned a lot about classical form and composition. He wrote the music for a theatre production of *Dangerous Liaisons* and has also written an animated feature film.

Being asked to compose the music for Emile's Kür provided an immense challenge for them, which they approached in a truly professional way. 'The first thing we needed was to get an idea of the kind of mood Emile wanted to create. We needed to see the choreography. The best way was to go and watch Emile ride Legrini. We spent some time with the horse. We spent time taking a video of the entire routine. We shot it from various angles because it was important also to get the visual picture of what it actually looks like from the judges' positions. This helped us to get the visual impact Legrini was making as he was performing the choreographed piece. We wanted to feel the emotions that the horse gave while he was moving. We also went to a couple of shows to see Legrini perform under different circumstances. We touched him and wanted to feel what it was like standing next to such a serene animal. The same applied to Emile. We needed to get a feel for him and how the two characters interacted.'

Once the video was shot, Lara and Neil spent hours in the studio watching the footage over and over again. 'Our work was quite mechanical at first. We

A dressage rider performing half pass in trot. This shot was taken with a very slow shutter speed to give a sense of movement.

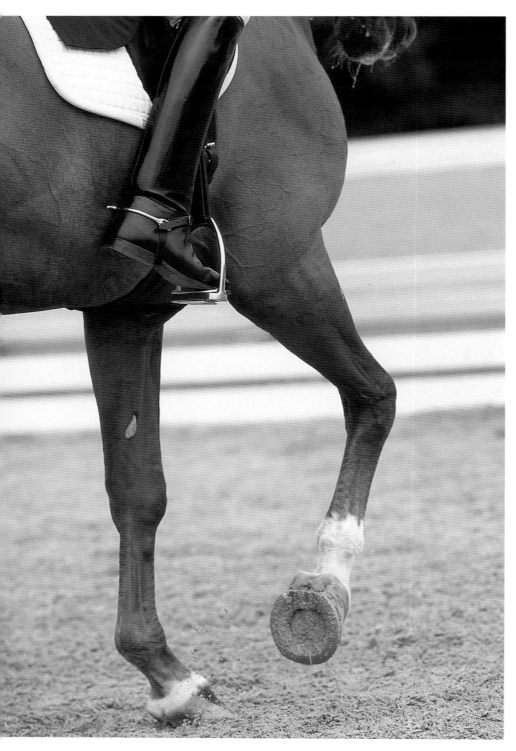

drew a column for the various movements the horse makes and a column for the sort of emotion each movement evokes. We logged the different moves and how long they took. Then we wrote down some musical ways in which we could achieve and accentuate or even dramatise the horse's movements.'

It is clear that music provokes emotions and watching every muscle change as the horse was moving, as well as watching the way Emile carried himself, gave the composers a source to draw from. 'We wanted to put a lot of emphasis on passion because we saw Emile and Legrini share that. We also tried to get some drama and romanticism into our piece. We treated the Kür like a ballet and felt the music should be part and parcel of one big package as opposed to a rider on a horse doing dressage to music.

'We took a baroque rhythm, with cellos, strings and a very high trumpet over the top. This, we felt, corresponded to the character and emotions of Legrini. The tempo changes were the hardest thing for us. The horse, thankfully, has to keep to a rigid time but the difficulty lay in the sudden changes of speed. We would be writing the music down for the canter across the diagonal and suddenly we felt a real explosion of energy. It was tricky to get these transitions right. The horse's power really comes across when you're watching it and we believe we have succeeded in matching our music to it.'

Neil and Lara agreed that the fine balance lay in getting the natural rhythm of the horse across but that the piece also had to flow. 'We needed to create the feeling of an ongoing movement through the entire performance. Even when the horse goes into a slower pace, there should be an "ongoingness" about it. We incorporated a few crescendi. They couldn't be too huge nor too loud. They are purely there to give the audience and the judges a sort of gut feeling that pulls the stomach up. A feeling of suspense and relief!'

Lara and Neil were slightly concerned that they couldn't compare their work to anything else except the cut-together pieces heard when visiting the Horse of the Year Show. However, when taking up the challenge, they were fully aware that their work could well help Emile to win a competition. 'We went into it almost blind. All we knew was that our music would be played alongside Michael Jackson and Beethoven and although we were fully aware that the music is not the most important thing, we didn't want the judges to feel obliged to shut their ears and minds to our composition! This is why we tried to keep the music as close as possible to the choreography. The tempo we gave it is not too rigid because we had to take into account that if the horse got slightly left behind the judges wouldn't get the feeling that the horse was completely out of time.'

Emile explained that he had choreographed the test around Legrini's strong points and therefore Neil and Lara also tried to accentuate those movements with their music. 'We knew that we could help to put across Legrini's strong points because although the judges are primarily watching the movements for their correctness, they will listen to the music at the same time. Part of our goal was to make sure that movement and music worked as one package.'

Composing this piece of music for Legrini and Emile was a totally new experience for Neil and Lara but one they mastered not only with formidable dedication but with true passion. 'It was a hairy one and a half weeks of working into the small hours of the morning and the pressure really made the adrenaline flow! Seeing it work was hugely gratifying. We would gladly do it again and because writing music is never the same twice, composing another piece for a Kür would lead to a new challenge.'

For those who have had the fortune to see Emile ride his Kür to Lara and Neil's music it is easy enough to acknowledge how well this specially composed piece works. For all the riders, regardless of the level they are competing at, who haven't, and who are still struggling to find effective music, I can only recommend the idea of talking to composers like Lara and Neil. If you do, your piece will be original, in keeping with the horse's character, very suitable and will run parallel with the choreography.

Neil and Lara were quite surprised that most top riders didn't put more thought into their choice of music. 'Top competitors are known to put a lot of hard work and dedication into perfecting their horses' movements and it would therefore seem only right to get the music as near to perfection as possible too. The paying audience, as well as the judges, expect quality and a polished performance. We feel that without a fantastic piece of specially composed music the picture wouldn't be complete. A specially written piece of music would suit the perfectionist attitude so many riders pride themselves on.'

Anky van Grunsven and Cocktail (NL), CDIO, Aachen 1995.

French rider Margit Otto-Crépin thoroughly enjoys riding dressage to music! While competing on Corlandus, Margit won the 1989 World Cup Final. Riding her German-bred partner Lucky Lord, Margit was placed second at the 1996 World Cup Final. At the 1997 Atlanta Olympics, the pair delighted the American crowd by choosing as their opening theme the title music of the hugely popular movie *Ghost*

Busters. Margit and fifteen-year-old Lucky Lord were seventh in the individual contest. Feeling the crowd's response and support not only brought a big smile to Margit's face, it also made Lucky Lord grow a few inches taller.

'I had a superb feeling when entering the arena in the freestyle. As soon as the spectators recognised the theme to *Ghost Busters* they went wild! This made me laugh because if you feel that the public feels the same way about your choice of music, you know that they will enjoy the test just as much as you do. I create my freestyle for the spectators. They have to appreciate it. This is exactly what happened in Atlanta and this is why I was so happy! I also believe that the music suited Lucky down to the ground.

'What I like most in a Kür is that I can express myself through my horse which I cannot do as much in the Grand Prix or the Special. I love music. It's a joy and a lot of fun to ride to music! Lucky Lord has a lovely honest character. He is a happy horse who likes to joke. He is a real tease in the stable. However, one has to be very careful not to be unjust with him. He doesn't like to be controlled. I have to be careful not to be too serious with him. I have to play more with him and be extremely light with my hands. Lucky really wants to please. However, he doesn't like it if I repeat a movement too often. He wouldn't want to do a pirouette five times in a row to get it perfect. I am better off trying it again at a later stage. This way I am sure to get his full attention as well as an improved movement.'

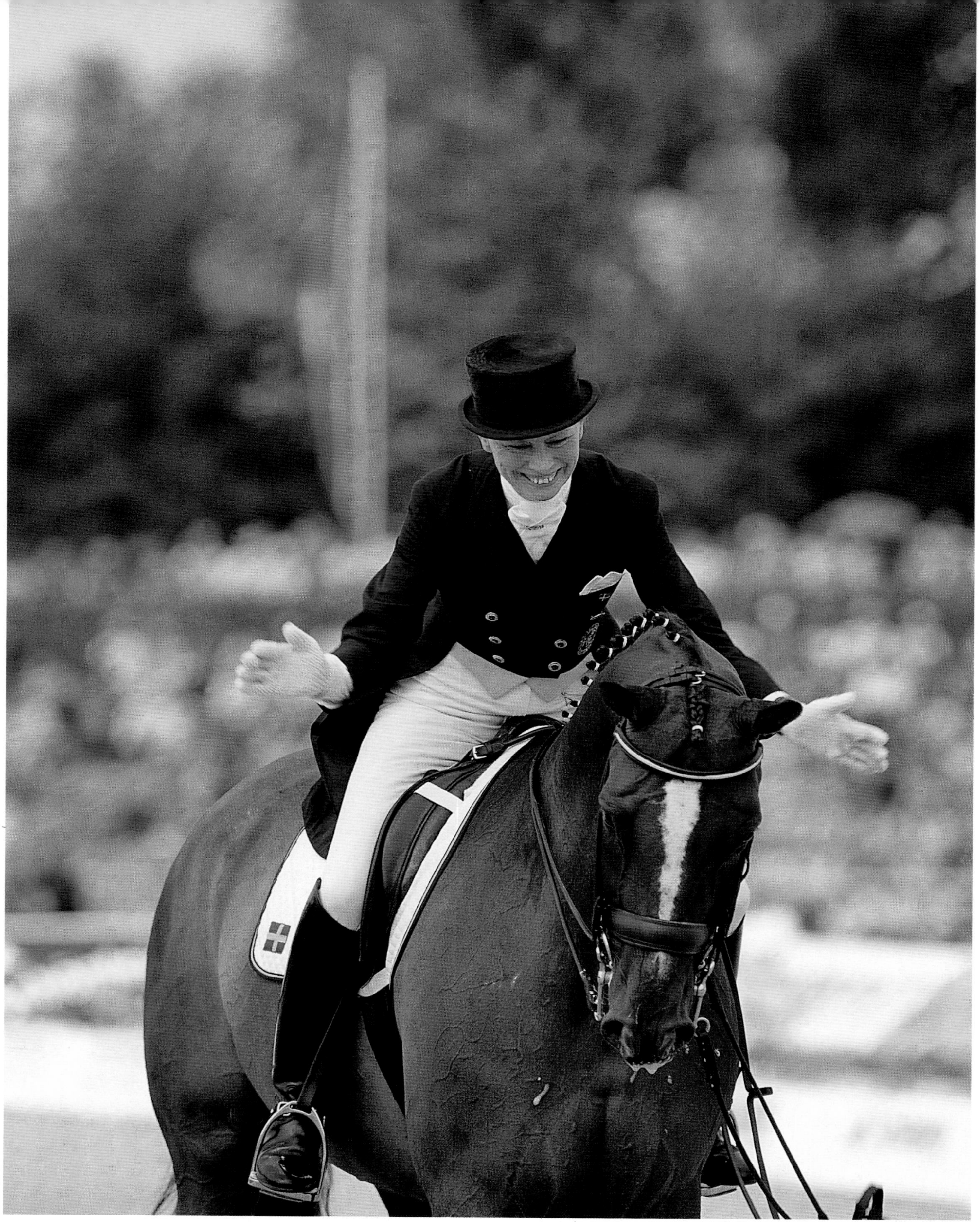

Swedish rider Louise Nathhorst and her Hanoverian gelding Walk on Top recorded their best season to date in 1997. In the spring they came third at the World Cup Final and in August they won a team bronze medal at the European Championships as well as being fifth in the individual contest. Louise, however, believes that Walk on Top's best performance was when they won the Stockholm World Cup qualifier in December when the twelve-year-old gelding scored a percentage of 79!

Louise bought Walk on Top in Germany as a seven year old and has brought him on to Grand Prix level together with her trainer/boyfriend. When preparing a Kür, the two also work on the choreography together. The music Louise rode to in Verden was, however, arranged by no less a musician than Benny Andersson from the hugely popular pop group ABBA! One of Louise's horse's trademarks is that he always has his ears pricked well forward! Here the two are pictured during their Kür in Verden as well as at the very end of it when Louise couldn't help but display her delight.

'It is difficult to explain what emotions I felt at this very moment. It is so fantastic when you know that you have just performed a really nice test where your horse has given his best and done everything you have asked him for! Walk on Top is such a sensitive horse and a really nice guy! He just gives me such a lovely feeling when I ride him. He loves to work and I feel that he is getting stronger and improves at every show. He has a fantastic character. When I first bought him not many people thought that he would be as high up in the world ranking as he is today. I always felt that our relationship would develop into a precious one. He does great flying changes and is good in passage. As for the extended trot, well it's just like flying! It's a fabulous feeling. Like taking off in a Boeing 747! He probably gives a little more in the arena than he does during a training session because I ask for a little more of him during a competition. In Verden it was just so much fun! I was so happy that we both managed to give our best.

'My philosophy is to enjoy every moment of it. Before I had Walk on Top I rode Dante. He had a bad injury just before the Barcelona Olympics and you never know when you might get another horse that can take you to the top. So I told myself that I was going to enjoy every minute because it can all vanish so quickly! Walk on Top is the horse of my life although I always thought that Dante was. But because I spend so much time with my horses they all become special! Walk on Top can be quite naughty. I can't put my groom on him and send them out on a hack because they would come home separately!'

Finnish rider Kyra Kyrklund has been based in Sweden, as consultant to the Flyinge Stud, for the past seven years. She has been National Champion of Finland more often than she can remember and hasn't been back to compete in the event since the mid-eighties so as to give other riders a chance. However, Kyra travels to Finland at least five times a years to visit her parents and to train the Finnish Juniors and Young Riders. On joining the stud, Kyra was given the responsibility of taking the Swedish warmblood stallion Amiral to Grand Prix level and of showing him. In his first international season Amiral was placed tenth at the 1995 European

Championships. In Atlanta he had the misfortune to injure his eye in the stable, which meant that Kyra could ride him only two days before their test. At the 1997 World Cup Final the pair were placed fifth.

Here Kyra and Amiral are pictured performing a canter pirouette, with Kyra holding both reins in one hand, during their freestyle at the 1997 European Championships. They were ninth in all three disciplines.

'Although I made a few little mistakes in the Grand Prix I was pleased with Amiral's performance. As for the Special, I think it was one of the best ones Amiral has ever done. The Kür was good, not spectacular but solid. I like the new formula at championships because all disciplines count. It means that horses and riders have to be consistent over three days. This eliminates having a lucky winner. I enjoy working on my Kür. A lot of riders use professionals to compose or arrange their music. I don't. I choreograph most of my tests alone and I choose my music myself. It is a lot of work and can get quite expensive but I like finding the right music and riding to it! Different horses need different types of music. I always want to express my horse's temperament so I look for a piece of music that will match my horse's personality. Amiral has quite a powerful character. I don't like lazy horses and Amiral is quite the opposite! Although he is a horse with a lot of nervous tension, he is never silly with it. He shows a very good front leg action and has a lot of expression. He learned all the movements with ease. If Amiral was a human he would be a theatre performer. He has so much presence. Further, he likes to travel and compete. He thinks that rehearsals are boring! He prefers to be on stage and in his case the arena is his stage!'

German-born Sven Rothenberger began riding for the Netherlands in 1994 when he took up Dutch nationality after marrying Dutch dressage rider Gonnelien Gordijn. While still riding for Germany Sven had won the 1990 World Cup Final on Andiamo. Since then he has consistently been placed either second or third in the same event. More recently, he took second place at the 1997 World Cup Final when riding the Hanoverian stallion Weyden. Here the pair are pictured performing a flying change, with Sven holding the reins in one hand, on the centre line during the freestyle at the 1997 European Championships. They were members of the silver-medal-winning team and came seventh in the individual contest.

Sven wasn't too pleased with his performance in Verden and puts it down to mismanaging his horse's season. 'First I rode Weyden at the World Cup Final, then at Aachen, then at the National Championships and finally at the Europeans. Other than that, Weyden had also covered a lot of mares this season and I think that by the time Verden came along he wasn't at his best. It simply wasn't our show and I'd much rather think back to the individual bronze medal we won in Atlanta! I also think that I rode the test of my life when we won the World Cup qualifier in Paris. Weyden was terrific and we scored a percentage of eighty one!

'Planing a Kür really is a lot of work! I only enjoy it if it pays off at the end of the day! Everybody knows how difficult it is to get a horse to Grand Prix level. Then one has to find the music and choreograph a programme that works well! However, I think that our sport simply has a far greater chance of reaching a bigger audience with the Kür. Further, if as a rider you feel at home in the freestyle, you have the possibility to improvise. I can adjust the test to how my horse feels on the day. And as my granny once said: "What is more boring than watching one Grand Prix? Watching two!". When preparing a Kür you are dealing a bit with the unknown which is exciting because you never know in advance how the judges or the public will take to it.

'As for Weyden, he is almost human! He is extremely intelligent and listens to my voice. I only have to tell him to stand up and he will stand square on all four legs! Weyden is definitely the best horse I have ever had. He is always in perfect equilibrium. He is exceptionally supple and shows superb elasticity.'

Grunox the mount of German
rider Monica Theodorescu
fully concentrated during
his test.

JUDGES

It is not unusual for international judges to sit together after a long day's work to compare notes and have a general chat about the outcome of a competition. Perhaps one of the judges was not quite in accordance with his or her colleagues? Perhaps one judge had a very valid reason for marking a specific movement differently to the way a fellow judge did? All of this, say the judges, is not as alarming as it may seem as long as it gets discussed. In the case of a difference of opinion, colleagues try to understand each other's views and learn from them. Often they will find that although they have a slightly different total, when comparing their sheets their comments are much the same.

To give high level dressage competitors the assurance that their tests are carefully watched from all angles, the five judges on duty are positioned at different points around the arena. Three judges are placed at the top of the arena: one at C, head on to the centre line, and two on either side of C, head on to the diagonals. The two remaining judges are situated half-way down the two long sides of the arena, one at E and one at B. This gives them a very good view of what is happening at X. Generally speaking, the judges at C get a better feeling of how the test is presented and the ones placed along the sides get a better sense of the horse's way of going. It is unusual for judges to have a favourite position around the arena. They maintain that the perspective remains of equal interest from any of the five angles. This is understandable because, after all, no matter where a judge is placed their prime duty is to give an open-minded yet critical view of what is presented in front of them. Besides, if it wasn't for having to fulfil a task which bears a great deal of responsibility, we could argue that judges are, in actual fact, really lucky because they most definitely have the best seats in the house!

Some international judges, such as Britain's Stephen Clarke, still get called to judge at Novice and Medium level, a job Stephen finds just as challenging and interesting as judging at the highest grade. When judging at the lower end of the scale, however, a judge's role becomes a rather different one. Less experienced riders, as well as more experienced ones on young horses, rely on the judge to offer criticism that will help them and their horses to improve. In the same way that a course designer sees his role partly as a trainer through his designing, so the Novice dressage judge aims to encourage and help competitors to progress. A good judge will mark horse and rider according to their standard of training and guide them along by means of marks and comments. A judge can let riders know if they are on the right track or not. In this way, performing in front of a qualified panel becomes another way of gaining knowledge and useful information. Ideally, by analysing their sheets, competitors will be guided towards improvement. Looking at the judge's remarks will help riders to take a closer look at themselves and their training method. If horse and rider show disharmony or incorrect movements, this will be reflected on the judge's sheets. Taking account of the judge's opinion gives competitors the opportunity to adjust their schooling at home before presenting themselves again at a later stage. No matter what level of competition they ride at, dressage riders all have the same goal: the desire to be in perfect harmony with their horse and to execute the required movements in a correct and effortless manner.

All riders like to see their tests marked in a fair, consistent and encouraging way. They welcome the fact that the judge's attitude has improved over the past few years. Judges are no longer as condemning as they used to be. The general feeling among competitors is that judges have become more open minded. They now show a much more positive approach and are keen to encourage horse and rider which, in turn, helps not only to keep the sport alive but makes it grow at a considerable rate. Riders agree that criticism is fine as long as people don't come away from a competition feeling depressed and completely put down.

Some riders, however, do still come away feeling slightly disheartened by the way their test has been evaluated, especially if they had a good feeling throughout the test. In this situation, however, it is not worth complaining. It could, after all, be purely a matter of a difference of opinion and, as long as it

doesn't happen on a regular basis, competitors just have to be philosophical about it. If, however, it occurs more frequently, it should be seen as an incentive for the rider to go home, work a little harder and come back again to see what happens next. Competitors have to be open minded too. If they are not, they won't get anywhere. They will just develop an attitude.

Talking to Novice riders, it transpires that they like having their test evaluated by judges who ride themselves. This gives competitors the confidence that the judge is familiar with the possible difficulties the rider might encounter during the test. They believe that, in this case, the judge's criticism will be more constructive.

International competitors, on the other hand, have the assurance that the panel of judges evaluating their performances are highly qualified for the job. Before becoming an Official International Judge, the person in question will have moved through the ranks of International Candidate Judge, followed by a period as an International Judge. During that time the judge will have gained immense experience by acting as a member of the ground jury at numerous international dressage competitions and will have attended several FEI (Fédération Equestre Internationale) courses. International Judges are appointed by the technical committee after consultation with the relevant national federation and are selected by the Bureau of the FEI. Similarly, an Official International Judge is also selected by the Bureau of the FEI on advice from the Standing Technical Dressage Committee, and then moves from being an International Judge to the status of an Official Judge which allows him or her to work at CDIOs as well as at championships.

In the following two interviews, Eric Lette, Chairman of the FEI Dressage Committee, and Official International Judge Stephen Clarke share their views and philosophies and explain the duties of their respective roles within the sport of dressage.

Stephen Clarke

'Judging a high pressured competition gets the adrenaline going because you are under pressure to get it right! It's as nerve-wracking as being on a helter skelter. One is slightly anxious at the start but it's a great feeling when you get off at the other end!'

International dressage judge Stephen Clarke has worked with horses from the age of seven when the owner of a nearby farm literally 'threw Stephen on board' to break in ponies brought over from Ireland. 'I was so frightened of the farmer that I didn't dare fall off!' After this initial introduction, Pony Club laid the basic foundation for Stephen's attraction to horses. It was also then that his love for horses became more and more apparent. 'The way horses move drew me to them right from the start. Just to watch horses in the field is most fascinating.' Stephen believes that seeing horses at liberty is very relevant to their training and recognises that observing horses moving as nature intends them to move touches him emotionally.

Although Stephen worked in the printing industry for a year, he soon realised that having a conventional job wasn't really for him and that a career with horses was foremost in his mind. He started his own yard,

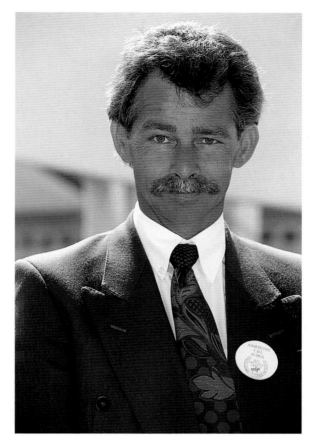

breaking in tricky youngsters that other people couldn't manage. 'I found that fascinating because it showed me that one connects with horses through their minds and that brute force just doesn't work.'

It was during his time at the Wirral Riding Centre that Stephen did most of his show jumping and eventing, competing at venues such as the Bramham Horse Trials, Hickstead and the Horse of the Year Show.

While Stephen may have started his competitive life in show jumping and eventing before taking to dressage, he remembers his curiosity about dressage from day one and says that the other disciplines 'just happened to have jumps in the way'. 'I have always been interested in the way horses use themselves so to specialise in dressage came as a natural progression.'

Stephen's interest in judging developed out of a rather frustrating experience he had while competing at a dressage show on one of his eventers. 'I had a particularly nice ride that day but when I received my sheet, I simply couldn't believe how negative it was. It was so depressing and demoralising that my immediate reaction was not to compete in the sport any more! But then I thought: "Hang on a minute! I like training horses and proving to myself that they will move correctly in an arena."'

From then on Stephen's motto was very clear: 'If you can't beat them, join them!' Further he thought, 'If everybody is getting as negative a sheet as I just did, we are not going to have a sport before too long!'

It was Stephen's passion for dressage that made him turn the encounter which upset him into the incentive to become a judge.

Although Stephen was still competing, and won six National Championship titles at different levels between 1982 and 1992, and was also reserve rider for the 1988 Seoul Olympics on Beckett, he simultaneously progressed to becoming a list-one judge, entitling him to judge nationally up to Grand Prix Special.

However, Stephen wanted to take his new vocation a step further. Through the recommendation of his own federation, who are able to put forward their applicants to the FEI, he became an FEI Candidate Judge in 1995 and a full International Judge a year later.

In 1997 the FEI promoted Stephen to Official International Judge which meant that he could now judge at CDIO shows as well as championships. Stephen feels very proud of his newly acquired title and spends at least two weekends a month judging in places as far away as Canada or even Japan. 'I like international shows very much, particularly the ones in the US because first one gets asked to judge the Grand Prix and then the next minute you find yourself sitting in front of a Novice class. It is fascinating to watch how horses develop through training.'

Stephen is well known for his sense of fairness and describes his approach to judging as realistic. 'I find judging quite difficult. You really have to use your brain and not allow yourself to get carried away into an unrealistic area by your emotions. If a horse that you don't like enters the arena, you have to be fair because it still might go round the next corner and, with a flick of a switch, perform a very good movement. I find it very important to really use the scale of marks in a justifiable way, not through emotions but just through "deservingness".'

Stephen believes that looking at the whole picture that unfolds in front of the judges' eyes helps him to keep an open mind. 'People often run into difficulties because they start looking too much at the details rather than allowing themselves to look at the entire picture, especially when a mistake occurs in a movement. I don't believe in giving a low mark simply because of a mistake. My reaction is to think of what I would give this movement without the mistake. Then I might have to come down a mark or so because of the

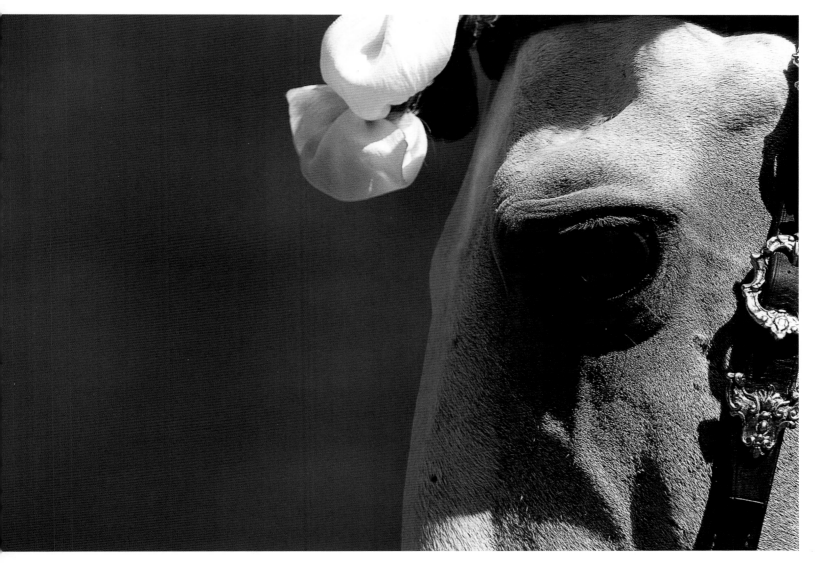

The Lusitano stallion Eleito, Britain 1997.

error. This is very important because all horses make mistakes. However, if one isn't careful, one can have a quality horse that has made a mistake on the same mark as a horse that is moving in a poor way. And this wouldn't be fair!'

For Stephen, a horse that is going in a poor way is one that shows stiffness, has dull paces, lacks expression and is on the forehand, as opposed to a well-trained horse that would not only be supple and well engaged but also carry itself well, using its hind legs. 'One can only see a horse's true potential when it's ridden in real balance and self-carriage. When I judge at national shows I notice that most horses are probably very nice but, unfortunately, there are occasions where their training hasn't allowed their potential to come through. Often, talented horses are

Jeanette Haazen and Ainsly Windsor (NL), CDIO, Aachen 1995.

rushed through their formative training and so they never reach their full potential.'

Stephen is very clear about the training scale that riders should adopt. 'Horses have to be made straight and they must react. It is so important for a horse to react to his rider and for the rider to react to his horse in the right way. It is all about forward movement. When you ask a horse to move forward it *must* move forward instantly from the slightest driving aid. When a horse doesn't, the rider starts pushing and shoving. The horse starts to push back which amounts to the end of his potential. Horses have to be free and in front of the rider. They must understand and be trained to understand the meaning of a half halt by the

use of transitions. Once the basic training has been established and the horse is straight, supple through his back as well as laterally and his weight is on his hind legs, you have a dressage horse that is ready to be developed.'

The importance Stephen places on the classical training principles is very much reflected in his judging philosophy. 'Mark up good training because good training leads to beautiful dressage. At the end of the day it is really all we have to consider if we want our sport to grow. We must appreciate that dressage is also watched by the general public. It is therefore worth bearing in mind that people who might not be very educated in dressage can still see if something is attractive to look at or not. I am after correct training which leads to beautiful dressage which leads to people wanting to watch. For me beautiful dressage is lightness, harmony, elasticity and impulsion, all performed without force. It is the development of natural gymnastic movement with a confident and willing horse.'

To ensure that competitors are judged as accurately as possible, the judges are placed at different positions around the arena. Generally speaking, the judges who are placed along the sides of the arena get a better feeling of the way the horse is moving, while from the front they will get a greater sense of the presentation.

'From E and B one tends to see a little more of the horse's frame, his degree of engagement and balance, whereas from C one has a better view of how accurately the figures are being presented. I don't really have any preference to where I want to be judging from. As long as I am sitting in a judge's box I am assured one of the best views in the stadium!'

Judging a large field of competitors demands a high level of concentration. If one is as dedicated to the sport as Stephen, however, it doesn't seem to be a problem. 'I am absolutely fascinated from the start of a class to the finish! I am so engrossed that every rider becomes a new challenge. Surely it is our job to train the mind to concentrate on what is happening without letting the point of focus wander to a previous or future pair.'

Another challenge judges have to meet is to look at every rider with a fresh set of eyes. 'It is very human to have a slight preconception of certain horses and riders simply because one has seen them before. However, one mustn't allow that to interfere with how a couple is actually performing on the day. We are trained right from the beginning to judge each movement as it comes. Actually, I am not concerned with who the eventual winner will be. What I am interested in is making sure to evaluate every movement of the test for its correctness. The winner will find themselves in that. And when one is working with a team of judges who react in precisely the same way, it's fascinating to see how close the marks are.'

When it comes to judging dressage to music, Stephen points out that the same classical principles of schooling, and therefore judging, apply. 'The compulsory movements are judged by the same criteria as they are in a straight test. I like judging the Kür. It is, however, more difficult because one also has to assess the choreography, the suitability of the music and the degree of difficulty shown. You have to be careful not to get carried away by the music. Beautiful music can lull the judge into possibly thinking a movement is nicer than it actually is. I always take care to appreciate clearly what is happening technically and to mark accordingly.'

Some riders perform certain movements by putting the reins in one hand which is judged, as Stephen points out, under the heading 'well-calculated risk'. 'So if a rider performs a movement and it works out, I go up a mark, but if a rider tries a movement and doesn't pull it off, I have to mark it down.' Stephen has judged Young Riders, Juniors and Pony European

Championships and was reserve judge at the 1997 Senior European Championships. Asked whether he has any special aspirations in his judging career, he says modestly, 'What comes comes. All I want is to keep improving. You learn every time you judge. It is like riding really. You are only as good as your last competition. You can never afford to be complacent or you are out of the game!'

Stephen is very clear on one goal though. 'For the sake of dressage we must all pull together collectively – riders, trainers, judges and journalists – because we are in it together. We must never forsake the classical principles. There is no danger in wanting to make dressage more appealing to the general public if we are clear about not compromising our principles of classical dressage. The main objective has to be that horses should always perform in as natural a way as possible and that the training should only develop and improve what nature has already given the horse, and all of this without abusing the horse either physically or mentally.'

Stephen is also adamant about not tolerating mistreatment. 'In ignorant hands there is abuse. In a judging situation I cannot tolerate that! And I don't!

'Judging means encouraging horse and rider. Telling them that they are on the right track but in a realistic way. I am not prepared to tell anybody that their test is good when it is not. Occasionally people think that I am too kind but I am not! I just want to keep my judging positive. I make a point of being realistic because I don't want to lead riders down the wrong path. If a test is good, I appreciate it. If it's not, then I am sorry.'

Eric Lette

'Choosing a career with horses, rather than becoming a lawyer, provoked more or less a scandal in my family. However, I have since been accepted again! My father, being an artist, had less of a problem with it.'

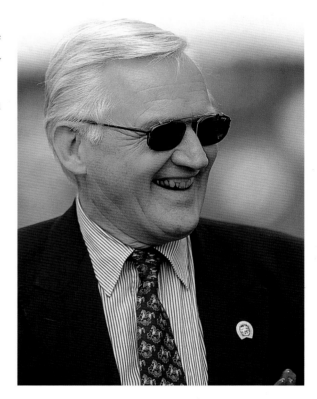

Swedish-born chairman of the FEI dressage committee, Eric Lette started to ride at the age of nine, became hooked on dressage as a teenager and decided to build his life around horses after having studied law at the University of Stockholm. During his five years of studying, Eric supported his passion by training other people's horses.

Eric puts his interest in dressage down to the fact

that he was fortunate enough to ride a horse of Grand Prix standard at a relatively young age. 'My horse could do one-time flying changes, piaffe and passage and, although I didn't perform them to perfection at the time, it gave me a feeling of what horse and rider were capable of achieving together. Being a teenager, I somewhat lost respect for dressage because, thanks to having a schoolmaster, I was able to experience all the high class movements.'

Although Eric had been a dressage trainer as well as a competitor, and had judged dressage at a lower level for some years, he was truly taken by surprise when the president of the Swedish Equestrian Federation told him that Eric's predecessor, Wolfgang Niggli, had suggested that he became the next chairman. 'I first met Wolfgang Niggli in 1986 when we tried to convince the FEI that Stockholm was capable of organising the 1990 World Equestrian Games. It was just a few months after our initial meeting that I heard that Wolfgang Niggli wanted me to succeed him. I really wasn't thinking about joining the FEI at the time. In fact, I had even given up judging for a while because I was too busy training and competing. However, I was told that before one could be considered for the post, one had to be an International Judge. From the moment I took to the idea it all went very quickly and it wasn't too long before I became an Official International Judge.'

Each chairman can hold office for two consecutive terms before he or she has to be replaced. 'I was re-elected in 1996 and the last general assembly I will chair will be in the year 2001. Prior to my first election,

I had been a member of the dressage committee for four years. By the end of my second term I will have worked for the FEI for twelve years and I believe that is ample!'

As Eric explains, the job of chairman is full of obvious as well as invisible tasks. 'A very important duty is the responsibility for the dressage rules. However, I see my commitment to educating the judges as eminent. If the judging is not good, it causes too many discussions. If riders, trainers and spectators are to respect our sport, it is of great importance that the judging be good! Another goal the FEI have set themselves is to make dressage a worldwide sport. We need all the countries we can get, especially as dressage is one of the Olympic disciplines which doesn't have too many nations with top class competitors. This creates a problem for us vis-à-vis the Olympic Committee. A lot of my work consists in developing the sport. I travel to many countries to hold clinics for judges, riders and trainers in order to give the lesser known countries a helping hand. This takes a lot of organising. Most people think that I judge purely at championships and Olympic Games but this is only part of my job! Each year I travel to all five continents to judge as well as to conduct training courses. I could send other judges who would do as good a job or an even better one than me but I believe that it is important for me to encourage and educate. Some countries show a great interest in meeting the chairman.'

It is also up to Eric to recruit judges from countries where dressage might not be so popular. 'For some

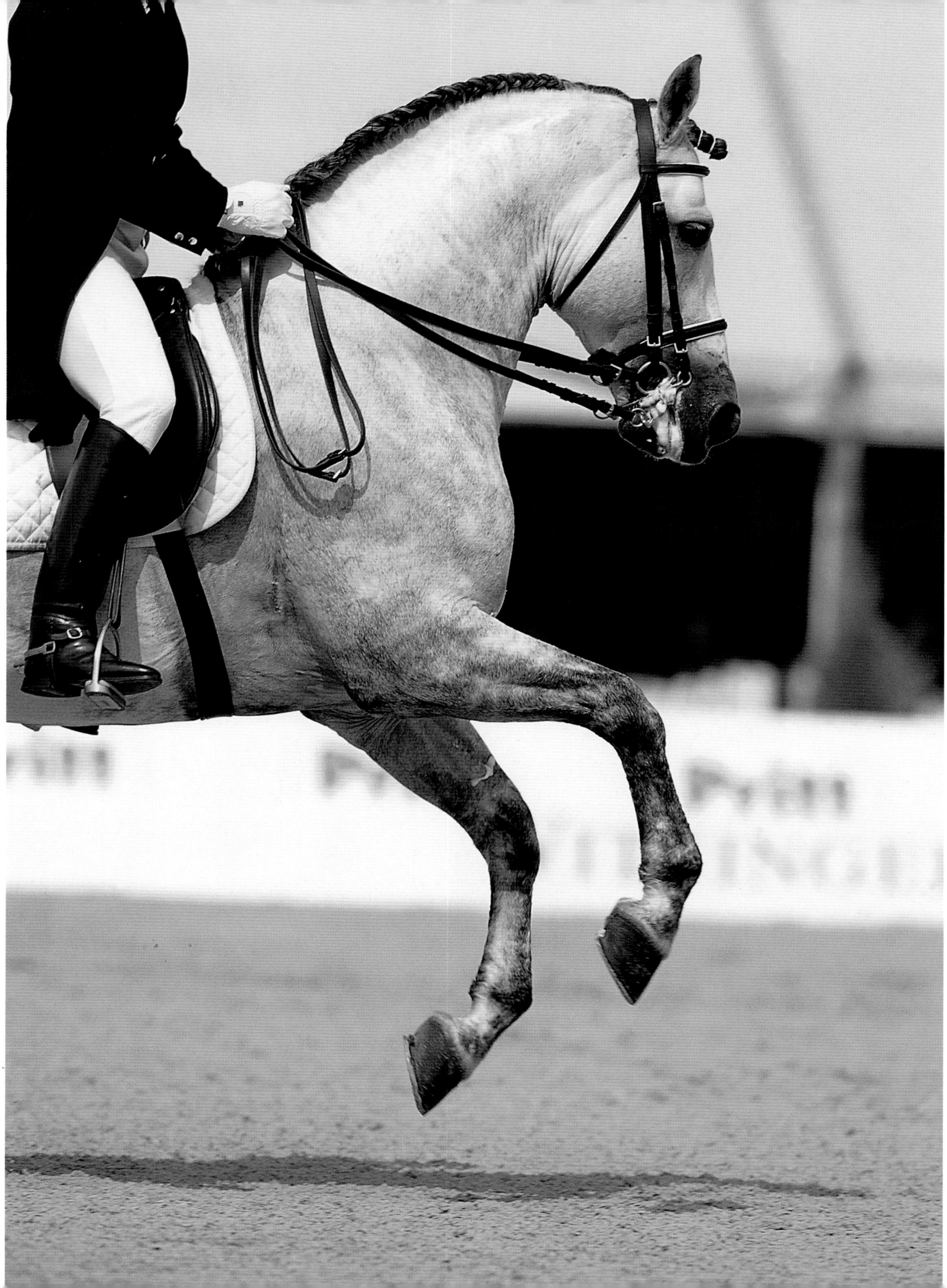

countries it is slightly easier to become a judge even if they don't have the experience that European or North American judges have. But it is imperative that we bring them in and that we list them as Candidate Judges because this is a way of communicating with them. Otherwise they would be outside the community.'

A lot of dressage enthusiasts believe that it is thanks to Eric Lette that the sport has seen some considerable changes. 'Yes, the judging has changed. I remember years ago, when I still competed, that judging was all about spotting mistakes and punishing horse and rider for them. I try to look at judging differently. My number one criterion is to look for quality. Once I have a mark for quality I will step up or down the scale depending on the technical correctness of the movement. Let's take an extended trot across the diagonal to elaborate my point. Here are horse and rider starting off on a nine. For a few steps at X they lose their rhythm. Towards the end of their extension their performance becomes a nine again. Years ago this movement would have fetched a four because regularity was very important – which it still is on the scale of education. However, if you have a horse that started with a six, made the same little mistake and had a six again, judges also gave it a four. In that way judges would punish a horse that showed more quality more severely than a horse that had less quality. I agree that the judge has to come down from a nine to an eight or seven because of the slight error. However, my point is that the two horses should not end up having the same mark! This is what I mean by judging quality first.'

Some years ago judges used to favour a certain type of horse. This trend has, however, disappeared under Eric's chairmanship. Eric is very clear in saying that: 'From a sporting point of view the ideal dressage horse has to be the horse that gets the highest marks in competition! I look for correctness in the movements and for the way in which the horse has been trained. I look for harmony between horse and rider. Horses have to be good movers. They have to be supple and show regularity in their paces. They have to be on the bit and push on with impulsion as well as having the right amount of collection. All of this is what I refer to as quality or self-carriage!'

One of Eric's most revolutionary achievements is undoubtedly the introduction of dressage to music into championships and Olympic Games. 'I must admit that this was very well initiated by my predecessor, Wolfgang Niggli. It started with the World Cup where we introduced the freestyle. When I wanted to introduce the Kür to championships and the Olympics, I came across a lot of resistance. It was really difficult because trainers, as well as riders, were against it. Today I am extremely pleased that everybody has accepted it. It is for all to see how necessary this innovation was. I am sure that in twenty years' time no one will remember what it was like riding without music! We are lucky that our sport lends itself to incorporating music. This gave us the opportunity to change. Other sports are not as fortunate.'

However, Eric is quick to point out that the people who were against dressage to music had a valid argument. 'Their concern was primarily that the

Ignacio Rambla and Evento (Sp), Verden 1997.

freestyle could turn into a circus act. We did take this on board. However, we always had the dressage rules firmly in mind and kept them alive for the Kür. We needed to remain true to the classical dressage and made small changes to ensure that it would not be like

artistic ones won't be high either. If a combination is not technically up to it, they cannot be artistic!'

Eric does see dressage as a form of art. 'Horse and rider create. It is for us, the spectators, to see. No horse and rider are the same which is wonderful! Dressage

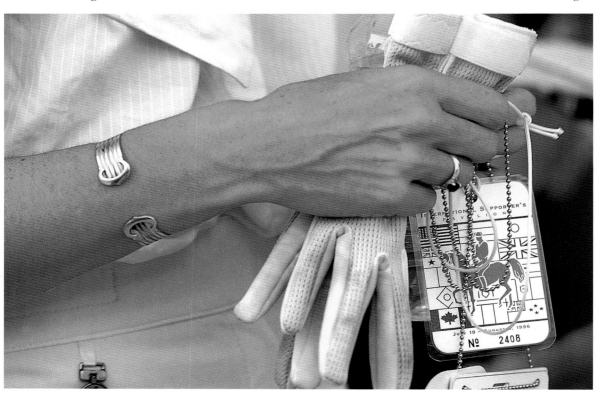

**Mary Hanna (Aus), Atlanta
Olympics 1996.**

a circus act. A lot of top riders were apprehensive. But today we have the proof that the riders who win the Kür are the ones who show exceptional performances in the Grand Prix and the Special. Another rule we made sure of was that riders could only qualify for the Kür through their performance in the Grand Prix or the Special. This means that we only see the best combinations in the freestyle. When judging the Kür, we put a lot of emphasis on the correctness of the movements. If the technical marks are not high, the

can look really good no matter how different the horses are. One horse can get high marks because of his lightness; another because of his power. I find these differences absolutely fascinating.'

So what is the fascination of judging? 'I don't know! I do question myself at times! It has to be due to the rewards I am getting from judging! My job offers me the opportunity to see the best horses and riders in the world and, together with my colleagues, we have the best seats in the house. We are positioned five metres from the arena, which means that we can really observe what is happening. Seeing tremendous horses and fantastic riding is what I interpret as my reward for the hours I put in.'

Judges are usually on duty from early in the morning until late into the afternoon. This is no different for the chairman of the dressage committee. Retaining one's concentration must be a key element to good judging. 'Keeping alert doesn't pose a great problem for me. It is slightly easier at the Olympics than at other big shows because, there, the field of competitors is restricted to fifty. It is, however, like in any other job, a matter of holding one's concentration. You have to approach it in a professional manner. I am just very conscious that I have to look at every horse and at every movement.'

After a class has been decided, Eric usually gets together with his colleagues to talk about the outcome. 'I have a lot of respect for my colleagues and when we have differences we discuss these. We talk about any point we might not have agreed on. This is the only way for us to learn from one another. As judges, it is very important that you look at things the same way so it's only natural that I want to find out why some judge has looked at a certain movement in a dissimilar way. I need to understand his or her judgement.'

However important the contest, Eric never shows nervousness when at work. 'I try to give my best. If people don't like my judging and should I no longer get invited, I will just have to accept that my judging might not be good enough. I do my job with pride and therefore I want to be a good judge. I feel proud if

riders are happy with my decisions. I do make mistakes – so do the riders – and I have to admit this to them and be humble. I am definitely not a happy man if I see that I have made an error of judgement. I can, at times, give too low or too high a mark. Now and again I don't agree with my

Anky van Grunsven (NL), Atlanta Olympics 1996.

fellow judges and at other times I realise that I was possibly too hard. When this happens I just think it over and try to do better next time.'

Eric sees a big advantage in being in contact with the competitors. 'It is highly valuable to communicate with riders and trainers. After all, we want to achieve the same goals – good sport and good riding. We therefore invite the representative of the riders' club, Christine Stückelberger, and the representative of the trainers' club, Herman Dukek, to some of our

committee meetings. There they have the chance
to voice their opinions. We are sure to have some
problems once in a while. It is impossible to keep
everybody happy at all times – winners aside – *they* are
always happy! Conflicts are inevitable and it is usually
down to me, together with the riders and trainers, to
solve them. However, conflicts are not always bad
because they generally bring us a step forward.'

The FEI has made considerable changes by taking
the riders' and trainers' views on board. 'Years ago
there used to be this big wall between riders and
judges. We have recognised that riders have an
influence and that it is our duty to listen to them.'

For Eric, good judging means that he is pleased
with the placings once the competition is over. 'This
doesn't imply that I give out the placings. I just give
marks for every movement. I never think of placing the
riders. That is up to the computer. However, if I have
the feeling that the panel of judges got the placings
right and that the best rider won, it makes me happy.

'I can only defend and explain every mark I have
given for a certain movement. People are misled in
thinking that we also give the placings. We never think
that one rider is better than another. It is not our
duty to compare riders. When you are judging thirty
to forty competitors it is impossible to compare what
you have given a rider for a walk pirouette early in
the morning to what you are giving in the afternoon.
The right way of judging is finding a certain standard
for each movement. We simply judge. We don't allow
ourselves to give a leeway for a better mark simply
because we know that a top contender is scheduled

to ride two hours after another favourite. We just
mark what we see and then it's over. Yes, we do mark
mistakes but we never forget that although a horse and
rider have made an error in one movement, it doesn't
mean to say that they cannot produce their next
movement brilliantly! Even a weak horse can have
some true highlights.'

Coming to a final mark when judging a pirouette
can be very tricky because, as Eric explains, there are
so many different things to look for in a single movement which, in the case of a canter pirouette, also
happens very quickly 'The principle is to look for the
quality of the movement. I want to see that the rider
can collect the horse because this is necessary for a
pirouette in order for the horse to turn almost on the
spot while cantering. I want to see that the horse can
keep his canter and that it is supple. This gives me
a picture that I could possibly mark up with an eight.
Then I also look for the correct flexion, which has to
be to the inside. I look at the size of the pirouette.
Even if the canter, as well as all the basics, is good,
but the pirouette is too big, I have to bring my mark
down for technical reasons.'

It is clear to Eric that the classical training methods
are of uttermost importance. 'In our sport we also need
to take care not to lose touch with the traditions that
horsemen have followed for hundreds of years. There
are institutions, such as the Spanish Riding School of
Vienna, who make sure to keep certain traditions alive.
The way we want to keep traditions alive in the sport
is by making specific rules. Primarily we want to see
horses move freely through their paces. We are aware

that it takes time to train a horse up to Grand Prix level. Horses should be given the necessary time. They should be allowed to mature and become true athletes. We are also conscious that horses change their way of carriage as the training progresses. An older horse will show more collection and will carry more weight on his hind legs than a young horse. For the piaffe, the passage or the pirouette the horse has to be strong enough to carry more weight on his hind legs. This also makes the horse lighter in font and more comfortable to ride. I am inclined to verbalise this in a very simple way. Man used to ride horses hundreds of years ago because it was a form of transport. Nowadays we ride for fun but to a certain extent riding has remained a form of transport. For me dressage riding is nothing else than a controlled and comfortable form of transport. The aim of every dressage rider must surely be to be in control of the horse and to be comfortable.'

Dressage judging is by no means an easy task and, as Eric points out: 'Judging has little to do with voicing an opinion. It is hard work. In a Grand Prix we give nine marks, often accompanied by remarks, within the first forty-five seconds!'

And Eric's philosophy? 'We should never forget that when dressage is performed well it is beautiful to watch. If we can raise the standard to an even higher level we will find it easier to fill arenas with spectators who might not be experts but who will enjoy the performance. It is the top riders who can make this happen. Their performances give pleasure to people who don't know an awful lot about dressage. Beauty

will always be recognised and appreciated. I would therefore like to see the standard improve. I have seen a lot of great horses over the years but the marks still don't reach eighty per cent in the Grand Prix. The better the horses perform the happier I will be! The

Carl Hester (GB), Addington 1995.

freestyle is important but I can enjoy a Grand Prix or a Special just as much because when it is as close to perfection as possible it is music to my ears! This did not happen only to me but to thousands when watching Nicole Uphoff-Becker and Rembrandt in Barcelona and Stockholm. Around the world people recognised that their performance was truly magnificent. I therefore believe that the best way of selling dressage is to aim for the highest possible quality!'

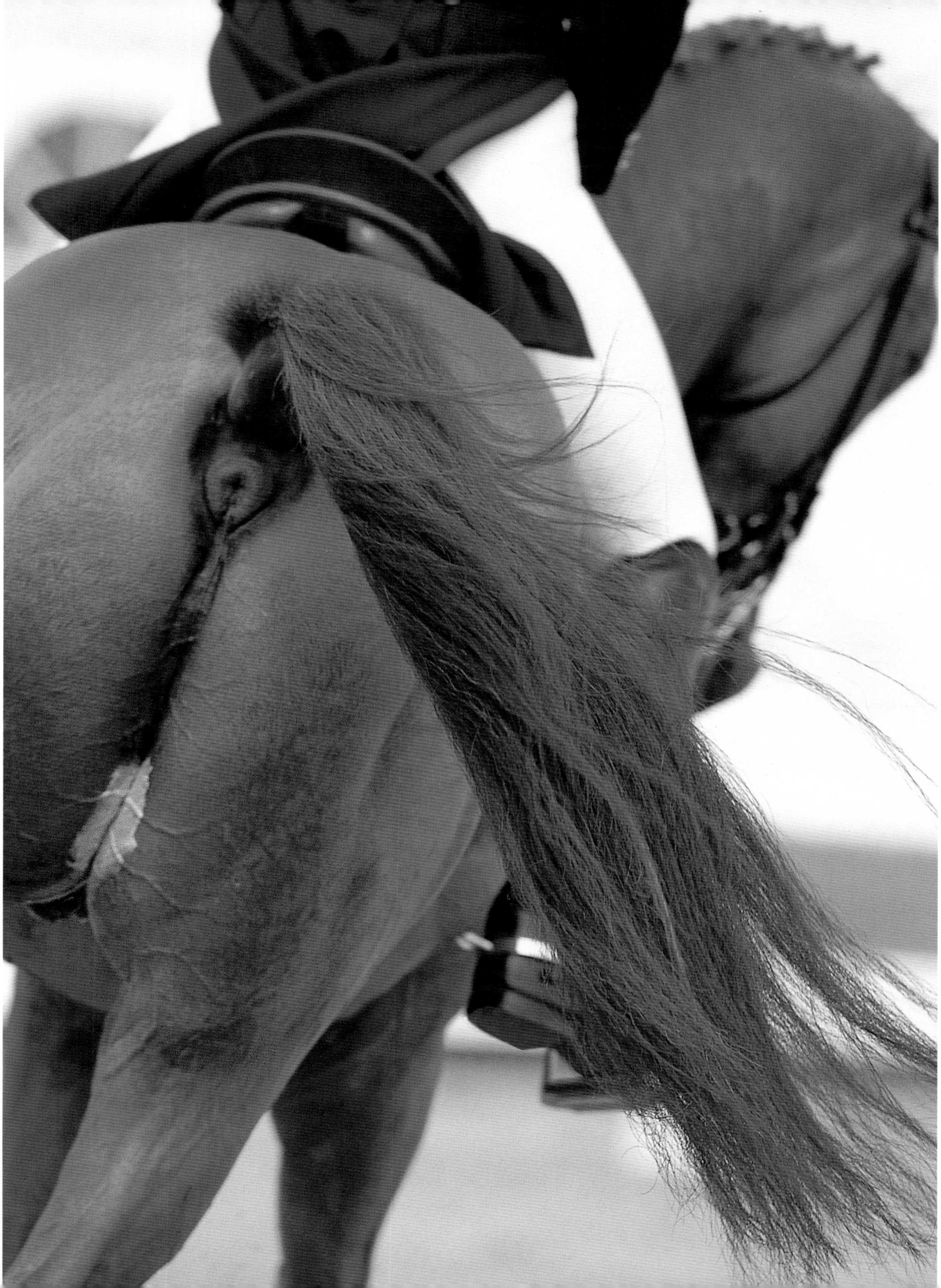

RECENT CHAMPIONS

When thinking of recent dressage champions, three ladies and their exquisite partners spring to mind immediately. First are Nicole Uphoff-Becker and Rembrandt for their remarkable Olympic success when the 21-year-old Nicole won the team as well as the individual gold medal in Seoul 1988. The Germans were quick to pick up on her achievements, noting that Nicole's win meant that she was the most successful dressage rider of all time when she became the youngest Olympic champion in her chosen field. It was an accolade which the pair matched in 1992 when they successfully defended both titles at the Barcelona Olympics.

With the Atlanta Olympics still firmly in everybody's mind, Isabell Werth and Gigolo are another obvious choice. Not only did Isabell go one better in the individual competition, winning gold this time as opposed to silver in Barcelona, she also secured her position at the top by winning team and individual gold a year later at the 1997 European Championships in Verden, Germany. Between Barcelona and Atlanta, Isabell and Gigolo became World Champions with the team and also individually by winning the Grand Prix Special at the 1994 World Equestrian Games in The Hague. However, Isabell was not the only one to be crowned individual World Champion that year. The FEI decided also to reward the best rider in the Kür to Music with a championship title in a separate event.

Completing my trio, therefore, are no less a pair than the Dutch specialists to music, Anky van Grunsven and Bonfire, World Champions of the Kür to Music at the The Hague World Equestrian Games. Anky and Bonfire underlined their supremacy in the Kür to Music by winning three consecutive Volvo World Cup Finals, from 1995 to 1997.

Dressage competition is both aesthetic and dramatic. The tension of finding out who is best on the day virtually fills the air during championships. These three ladies and their partners know all about coming to terms with nervous tension, pressure and stress. It takes a lot of discipline, hard work, self-control and determination to achieve what only a few can accomplish, namely individual titles. They work their horses day in, day out, trying to refine and perfect the highly skilled movements that competitors have to demonstrate in the tests at high-level international events.

Victory also depends on finding the right ally for the job. All three lady riders refer to the horses who have helped them to realise their goals not only as highly talented animals but also as friends with an exceptional character. They admit to knowing them better perhaps than any human friends they have.

Nicole Uphoff-Becker and Futurus (Ger), CDIO, Aachen 1996.

This doesn't come as much of a surprise if you take into account that riders spend hours first in getting to know their horses and then later in training them. Going through the ups and downs of a sporting career is bound to create a special bond between horse and rider. All rider and horse teams are trying to reach this 'oneness' and complete understanding, yet only a few succeed on a regular basis. On several occasions many competitors may create a harmonious picture, when the finest of aids were understood by their horse, but was this when it mattered most? Did all fall into place during the Grand Prix Special when the critical eyes of the judges were firmly focused on their performance? Were horse and rider at their best for the duration of an entire championship? The rewards go to those who are the most consistent over the whole championship period. Competing adds another dimension to skilful riding. It means putting into practice movements which you and your horse have executed beautifully at home where the surroundings are familiar to your horse. At the championships, competitors still strive to ride

Gigolo, Verden 1997.

with skill but, depending on his temperament, a horse can easily be put off by strange surroundings. Coming to terms with all the external problems, together with the individuality of each horse, is what makes a champion.

Putting this chapter together was easy enough. The results over the last few years speak for themselves. My only concern, however, is that men may feel slightly left out. To console them it is only fair to remind ourselves that German rider Dr Reiner Klimke won the individual gold medal at the 1984 Los Angeles Olympics and that Klaus Balkenhol was a member of the victorious German teams in Barcelona, The Hague and Atlanta. Further, German-born rider Sven Rothenberger, a member of the very strong Dutch team since 1994, is never far down the placings and produces remarkable individual results as well as when with the Dutch team. In Atlanta, Sven won an Olympic silver medal with the team and was placed just below Isabell and Anky when he brought home the Olympic individual bronze medal.

Nicole Uphoff-Becker and Rembrandt

'The challenge of dressage is to become one with your horse. It fascinates me to try and create the feeling of merely having to formulate a thought and then notice that my horse does what I have asked for. I love to feel that my horse and I are melting into one another.'

The triple German National Champions of 1988, 1989 and 1993, Nicole Uphoff-Becker and the formidable Rembrandt have demonstrated this affinity at almost every outing. The pair have enchanted judges and spectators around the world and boast numerous championship titles to prove it. After a rocky start to their career – 'Rembrandt used to tank off with me across the arena without warning' – the two got to know each other better and better and soon formed a tremendous partnership. Winning the 1987 European Young Riders' Championship with the team, as well as taking the individual gold medal, was simply the beginning of a series of titles that were to follow.

Their first major challenge came when the pair were chosen to represent their country at the 1988 Seoul Olympics. Nicole, only 21 years old at the time, showed no signs of being nervous. Although she won the gold medal, both with the team and individually, Nicole struggles to remember a single thing about it. 'It's really strange but I can only remember little events that happened in the stables or the Olympic village! I simply can't remember the feeling I had when riding my tests!'

Such a statement seems hard to believe because Nicole considers her assertiveness when riding as one of her most valuable assets. 'I am very self-critical and

will often notice that the horse is not performing at his best due to my mistake. I have taught myself over the years to be as aware as possible. I am concentrating throughout every step my horse takes and can therefore recognise if, say, I am not sitting straight and

Nicole Uphoff-Becker (Ger),
CDIO, Aachen 1995.

admit that the horse has made an error because of my position. Every rider should be assessing himself at all times. One is, after all, left to one's own devices when riding in front of the judges.'

Riding before a panel of qualified eyes brings another dimension to dressage. 'I have a healthy attitude towards competition and see it as a further challenge. It simply isn't enough to have a wonderful feeling at home or when warming up before the test. Somehow, I do need to prove to myself that the horse and I can achieve perfect harmony when it matters most. It can be very frustrating when your horse goes beautifully just before entering the arena and you

the moment when we reached the corner before the extended trot across the diagonal. Remmy just grew a metre taller in front, started pushing from behind and threw his legs forward. I am sitting there thinking: "But I haven't done anything, I have only thought it."

Nicole Uphoff-Becker and Freudenstänzer (Ger), CDIO, Aachen 1995.

simply can't recreate the same unity in front of the judges. However, when the affinity is there during the test it is an amazing feeling!'

One of these unforgettable moments happened during the 1992 Barcelona Olympics, when Nicole and Rembrandt successfully defended both titles won in South Korea four years earlier. 'The feeling Remmy gave me was unbelievable. You have to recall

Then came the very last extension followed by the circle in piaffe to passage. Watching it on video you can see that I had no strength left but I kept on saying to Remmy, "Come on, you can do it, just don't stop now!" And we made it! He just kept his rhythm. It was such an uplifting feeling. It literally moved me to tears and still does every time I watch the video!'

The same thing happened when nineteen-year-old

Two years after winning their first Olympic gold medals (team and individual) in Seoul, Nicole Uphoff-Becker and Rembrandt clinched top honours at the inaugural 1990 World Equestrian Games held in Stockholm's Olympic stadium. Nicole rode with her left hand in plaster which meant that she had much less control over her somewhat exuberant partner. 'This win meant an awful lot to me. Not only because Remmy and I managed to prove that we were still the top contenders but because Remmy behaved so beautifully when he could just as well have told me: "You can't use your hand properly so I'm not doing it!"'

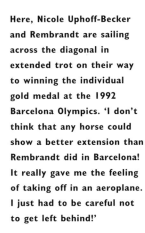

Here, Nicole Uphoff-Becker and Rembrandt are sailing across the diagonal in extended trot on their way to winning the individual gold medal at the 1992 Barcelona Olympics. 'I don't think that any horse could show a better extension than Rembrandt did in Barcelona! It really gave me the feeling of taking off in an aeroplane. I just had to be careful not to get left behind!'

Rembrandt and Nicole competed at one of their last shows in 1996, prior to the horse's retirement which they had already agreed upon. 'I was competing and the feeling he gave me then was even better than ever before. I could feel his hind legs reaching as far under his belly as possible. No three year old could have thrown his toes higher at an extended trot! The moment I was experiencing this marvellous movement, the thought that I was only going to have such a feeling another three times before we retired him entered my mind. I started to cry in the middle of the test, thinking that I couldn't carry on. One of the judges, Mrs Eisenhart, looked out of her little hut and, noticing how emotional I was, she started crying too!'

Watching Rembrandt and Nicole perform moved thousands of people around the globe. It was

Rembrandt's presence, elegance, grace and the refinement of his movements that caught their imagination. And it is the special bond that the two share that made their performances look so effortless. Nicole admits quite freely that needing to understand Rembrandt was the key to their partnership.

'I owe all I know now to Rembrandt! He has taught me to listen carefully to what he had to tell me. Rembrandt showed me, for example, that I shouldn't demand too much of him right up to the last minute before the test. I also remember coming back from his first big show. He was only nine then. When I sat on him the following day he felt flat and lethargic. I worried because it was so unlike Rembrandt. I got the vet, had blood tests done, the lot. All seemed fine and the vet suggested that Remmy was just very tired.

I couldn't get him to go forward for a whole week. On the seventh day he bolted off through the arena with me. Remmy was back! It was his way of telling me that he needed a rest after a strenuous competition and that *he* would show me when he was ready to work again! Decisions were so often his.'

However, Rembrandt also did his fair share of listening to Nicole. This became most apparent when they won at the 1990 World Equestrian Games held in the Olympic stadium in Stockholm. Nicole had broken her arm only four weeks prior to the championships and was competing with a cast round her left wrist. 'I had absolutely no strength in my arm and Remmy could have taken full advantage of it. But somehow he knew. He felt the importance of the competition and behaved beautifully. He grew tall the minute

we entered the arena and made me feel how much he wanted to perform well. It was unbelievable! Rembrandt is a great one for recognising big moments.'

Rembrandt showed his exceptional talent and intelligence in the way in which he learned the required movements. 'Teaching Remmy piaffe and passage was really easy. Once he was elevated I only had to hold him in front and he started to piaffe under me. The only difficulty I had was to keep his exuberance under control. But when it came to teaching him all the different movements, they were all very natural to him. He really didn't have any weaknesses. His transitions were just magical. He kept his rhythm beautifully from piaffe into passage. It was just like sitting on a metronome. The same with his half pass. I only had to set him up and he would do the rest. He was

Nicole Uphoff-Becker and Rembrandt warming up before their test at the 1994 CDIO in Aachen. Nicole has developed her own way of loosening up her horses in training. 'The idea is to free the horse's back and to develop those back muscles. The back has to come up and the horse's head and neck have to stretch downwards. Horses feel so much better once they have had a good stretch and their muscles are loose.'

difficult to sit on in an extended trot though. He really used himself and needed to feel free in his back. As soon as I would sit into him he wouldn't give me the same trot.'

Riding other horses can be quite tricky when you have been spoilt with a horse that can, and wants, to do everything. 'It is mostly when I ride horses with a problem that I just wish I could sit on Remmy again! I catch myself trying to recreate the same feeling I had on him when riding other horses, primarily because it is my aim to feel at one with any horse but also because I believe that it

German trainer Harry Boldt helped Nicole from before the Seoul Olympics until after the World Equestrian Games at The Hague. 'Harry and I got along exceedingly well. He has this marvellous calmness. He used to let me ride in my style and I could just get on with it. When there was something he needed to convey, I stopped and we would discuss it.'

is a great picture for spectators to see.'

Although Nicole has had a number of trainers, such as Schulten-Baumer, Harry Boldt and, more recently, ex-team mate Klaus Balkenhol, she reckons that a lot of what she knows is self-taught. 'Having the right trainers is very important. However, I can't stand having somebody around every day. Harry was very quiet which worked well for me. If things were good he simply nodded. If a movement wasn't right, he would

signal for me to come and we would talk it over. We had a very good rapport and stayed together from before Seoul until after The Hague. Now Klaus comes three to four times a month and that is really all I need. I have developed a great deal of sensitivity over the years and feel what the horses are doing.'

Generally speaking, Nicole hardly shows any signs of nervousness before a competition. She does, none the less, admit that having someone around at shows, does have a slight effect on her. 'In Seoul I drove everybody crazy because I was so calm. I wanted to have Remmy as relaxed as possible before starting to ask him for any specific elements. Everybody was permanently encouraging me to start on parts of the test. I kept on insisting that Remmy wasn't ready! I knew him best and there was no doubt in my mind that he wouldn't do anything correctly unless he was one hundred per cent loose. To achieve that I usually had to take him out for the first time for half an hour, four hours before our scheduled start. Then I used to put him back only to ride him again for an hour before the test. Sometimes that meant getting up as early as four in the morning!'

Again, it was Rembrandt who taught Nicole to stay cool, calm and collected before big championships. Things could get slightly frustrating when nerves or tension did creep in. 'I had to find a way of calming myself down because if I was nervous Remmy would feel it and simply go bananas! I used to try and find a quiet place and managed to bring my pulse way down. I thought of this myself and it was only much later that someone told me that I was practising self-hypnosis.'

When asked how she reacts when she feels that her performance has been undermarked, Nicole was quick to point out that it can cut both ways and that, in any case, she wouldn't want to trade places with the judges. 'Of course, it has happened that I felt the judges didn't give me the marks I thought corresponded to the sensation the horse gave me during the test. But, to be fair, I have also been in situations where I felt that the judges gave me higher marks than I deserved. I believe that it happens because of the positions the judges have when viewing the test. You often see the three judges at C giving the same marks and the two on either side of the arena giving different ones, or the other way round. I suspect that the angle the judges view the test from can be the reason for their differences. The few times I did feel undermarked, I was a little sad at first but, then again, the main thing is for you to feel happy with your horse's

Nicole Uphoff-Becker and Rembrandt performing one-time flying changes at the Barcelona Olympics, another movement Rembrandt excelled at. 'Remmy never had a problem with any of the movements. He just didn't have any weaknesses. The only difficulty I had was to keep his exuberance under control!'

Nicole Uphoff-Becker waving to the crowd before receiving the Olympic gold medal for her individual effort at Barcelona. 'I felt hugely relieved at this point! The feeling that overwhelmed me was that I had finally made it. There is so much pressure. One rider copes with it and the next doesn't. At the end of it all I was simply elated!'

performance. All in all, I really can't complain and I take these things in my stride. I have also been asked to judge and I can assure you that is a very difficult task that I don't want to be doing too often.'

When it comes to Nicole's thoughts on the Kür to Music, she explains that it does involve a lot of work, mainly because she doesn't consider herself a great choreographer. 'A lot of my likes or dislikes about dressage to music depend on the horse I am riding. Grand Gilbert went superbly to music. As soon as the music started, he found a rhythm and danced to it. He was simply very musical. With Remmy, however, I hated it! He used to always do his little side steps so we constantly ended up having to run after the music which was very stressful! One just has to have the right horse for it.'

Nicole says that although she can see the benefits the Kür to Music has with regards to its spectator value, she is an absolute fan of what she considers to be 'the classical competition'. 'I find it more real when every competitor is faced with the same task like in the Grand Prix. In the Kür, a rider can put more emphasis on the movements his horse does best and show the weaker points only once or twice, as well as placing them in a less visible position for the judges.'

Rembrandt, the partner Nicole refers to as 'the professor', shared similar views on the subject for, at the 1996 Atlanta Olympics, their last big outing before his retirement, he wasn't one hundred per cent sound before the final Kür. 'I wasn't too upset about it because throughout his career it was always up to Remmy to make the decisions. He decided when he wanted to work and when he didn't. In Atlanta he told me, "No, come on, enough is enough!"'

Now that Rembrandt is in retirement, he enjoys being turned out and receiving visits from his ever-adoring public. His character hasn't changed a bit. He

still calls the shots by deciding who he is going to turn around for in his box. 'He often wouldn't come and talk to me but not too long ago Remmy absolutely fell in love with a little blonde girl. He gazed at her adoringly and was visibly sad to see her go. When out in the field, it is also Remmy who decides when it's time to come in. He will always have a very strong personality and expect no less than VIP treatment.'

Here Nicole Uphoff-Becker is seen in an unfamiliar position during the prizegiving at the 1994 World Equestrian Games, where the top award went to Isabell Werth and Nicole had to settle for silver. However, Nicole and Rembrandt did win a team gold medal, thus holding on to a title they had already won four years earlier. 'I honestly have to say that Isabell and I have a good relationship. We are not best friends because one can call very few people that. However, we are very open with one another and we have a great deal of respect for each other's riding abilities.'

Isabell Werth and Gigolo performing a flying change on their way to securing their individual gold medal at the 1997 European Championships. 'Gigolo is so keen at a show. So far he's never let me down when it mattered most!'

Isabell Werth and Gigolo

Although Isabell Werth had already been very successful on horses such as Weingart and Fabienne early on in her career, she simply never left the winners' enclosure once she teamed up with the charismatic chestnut gelding Gigolo.

'When I sat on Gigolo for the very first time and I felt him move I knew deep down that he was the horse for me! I immediately felt a sense of belonging and that we were made for one another. However, the proof that Gigolo could truly mature into a Grand Prix horse and that we would blossom into the successful pair we now are, was down to time. Each passing year we learned more from one another and grew closer and closer.'

It was 1991 when Isabell and Gigolo first hit the headlines. Not only did they win two European gold medals (team and individual), but they won their individual title by beating Rembrandt and Nicole Uphoff-Becker! The same year the two also went on to secure the first of their four German National Championship titles (1991, 1992, 1995 and 1996). At the 1992 Barcelona Olympics they won the team gold and the individual silver medal, leaving the full honours once again to Nicole and Rembrandt. However, Isabell and Gigolo have never looked back since and have won every available title with the team as well as individually: the European

Championships in 1993 (Grand Prix Special as opposed to the Kür), 1995 and 1997; the World Championships of 1994 (Grand Prix Special); and the Olympic Games in Atlanta in 1996!

Isabell believes that coming second in Barcelona

taught her a lot and helped her to develop into the true champion she now is. 'In 1991 I went into the European feeling completely inhibited and almost naive. I had nothing to lose. In Barcelona things were different. I was suddenly among the favourites and expectations were high. The Grand Prix went very well but then little things, like a lot of noise during the warming up phase and Gigolo getting more and more

Isabell Werth and Gigolo in extended canter during their test at the 1994 World Equestrian Games in The Hague. After winning two gold medals (team and individual) the year before at the European Championships in Lipica, Isabell and Gigolo proved their supremacy by winning the team as well as the individual World Championship titles. In The Hague there were still two individual titles to be won: the one in the Special, which Isabell won, and the one in the Kür which went to Anky van Grunsven.

nervous, made me lose my cool. At the time I just couldn't cope with disturbances I am very capable of ignoring now. Nicole and Rembrandt gave the performances of their lives over the three days and I made silly mistakes. As athletes, both horses had the same chances but when it comes down to winning the Olympic gold medal it is the one who makes the least errors who wins. However, I learned to lose although I was among the favourites. It taught me that life goes on and that the world doesn't collapse! I was second but still alive. Yes, sometimes one believes that it's better to die than to be second! But I know of a good saying: "If you want to win you have got to be prepared to lose." Foremost, however, Barcelona taught me to fight on.'

Isabell Werth and Gigolo during their training session on the morning of the freestyle at the 1997 European Championships. Isabell usually takes Gigolo for his first outing a few hours before their test. 'We practise some of the movements so that Gigolo knows what lies ahead of us. Before the actual test I only ride him for a maximum of half an hour. I see no point in drilling a horse before his performance.'

Isabell had to dig deep into her fighting spirit in Atlanta and again in Verden, when lying behind Anky van Grunsven on both occasions, before the cards turned in her favour. 'The degree of tension I feel is closely linked to the importance of the test. I think that this is necessary in order to achieve a good performance and a high level of concentration. I need to feel a certain nervous tension. However, one has to be careful not to let it transmit to one's horse. I truly believe that a great performance can only be achieved in conjunction with a healthy degree of nervousness and tension. In Atlanta I had two dreadful days when I thought I had lost the gold medal because of the one test. But somehow I regained my spirit to fight on. We just kept on training calmly and peacefully because I knew that Gigolo was actually on top form. I can't explain whatever it is that actually makes me kick into gear. It is just an incredible challenge. I simply shut off everything around me. My tension rises and I detect a certain aggression in myself but not in a negative way. It is simply that I want to attack. I want to give my best performance. However, the more experienced the horse and the more united one is with one's horse, the greater the chances of realising that goal. It therefore really does take two and Gigolo is a fantastic ally!'

However, Isabell points out that Gigolo can become overexcited on the first couple of days at a championship. 'He is often on the verge of exploding even if it doesn't show. He is just so keen, which means that we are often treading such a fine line and it is up to me to get him spot on for the ten minutes we are in the arena.'

Asked whether Gigolo was difficult to ride, Isabell was quick to point out that most horses of Gigolo's calibre are bound to be somewhat tricky because they all have strong personalities. 'No, Gigolo is not a difficult horse. On the contrary, he is a true sportsman and a fabulous athlete. Riding him feels a bit like coming home because we know each other so well. We share a very emotional bond. I feel that it's my duty to try to keep him happy and enthusiastic.'

For Isabell dressage means achieving perfection throughout a given sequence of the horse's natural movements. It means accomplishing the most challenging movements with the greatest possible ease without anyone ever noticing the rider's aids. 'Dressage should genuinely be a coming together of horse and rider. I believe that I have actually accomplished this with Gigolo, not only because I have attained the finest successes with him but because we

are so close. I don't really want to humanise it but we really form a partnership where one knows the other inside out.'

The third element in Isabell and Gigolo's success story is undoubtedly their trainer, Dr Schulten Baumer, owner of all the horses Isabell competes on. 'My trainer is of uttermost importance! Without him I would never have reached the top and, furthermore, I would never have stayed up there! Fortunately, I live only five minutes away from Dr Schulten-Baumer's yard and he has known me for a very long time. When I started riding there it was just like being in heaven! At that point his children were still competing successfully and I felt it was a fantastic opportunity for me to watch and learn. Some eleven years ago the doctor asked me to ride for him and I was overjoyed. We are a fabulous team. He buys young horses, which is a big investment because it means purchasing 'hope'. We train them together, bringing them up through the ranks, which always includes overcoming lows and solving problems. But we never give up. We treat all the horses as children that we try to raise together.'

Isabell Werth and Gigolo on their opening trot during the freestyle at the 1997 European Championship in Verden. The pair were just a fraction of a point behind Anky van Grunsven before the Kür. Gigolo did everything Isabell could possibly ask for during their final test, which helped them to clinch the individual honours to add to their team gold medal of the previous day. 'Gigolo was incredibly attentive right from the start of our programme. He gave me a fantastic feeling during the entire test. Gigolo is fabulous to ride because I am so sure of his ability and confidence.'

Isabell Werth and Gigolo
trotting around the outside
of the arena before their
Grand Prix Special at the
1994 World Equestrian Games.
Riders are allowed a few
minutes to familiarise their
horses with the surroundings
of the arena before they are
asked to commence their
performance. Here Isabell
is asking Gigolo for a final
extension before embarking
on the ride that won them
the individual gold medal.

Isabell finds the training of young horses very satisfying and wouldn't miss it for anything in the world. 'Riding the youngsters is a real treat. To feel them move, getting to know them and experiencing the gradual shared acceptance of one another is wonderful. The first three to four years are based on growing together and on overcoming the ups and downs. Taking them to their first shows is terribly exciting. Competing with them on the small circuit truly is the reward for the previous years. I can't say that all those years are hard work. In fact I can't put into words how happy I am when a youngster does his first flying change or his first steps of piaffe! Yes, there are phases where nothing seems to work and doubts creep in. This keeps me awake at night, thinking about what I might have done wrong but when the horse actually makes it to Grand Prix, it's the icing on the cake!'

However, Isabell also needs the challenges that are associated with competing at the highest level of her chosen sport. 'Because I have made it my goal to produce a horse and get it to the top it is only natural that I would want to measure my performance against that of other riders. I need to know how good I am in comparison to the rest of the world. I thrive on the thrill competing gives me.'

Gigolo has grown into the splendid partner Isabell needs. Although for a time the pair made little mistakes on big occasions, Gigolo has become a much more mature horse. 'He has improved tremendously over the last two years and I believe that he has given his best performances at the Atlanta Olympics and at the European Championships in Verden. 'Because the 1997 European Championships were in Germany I especially wanted to do well. I was possibly too motivated and this is why I made a hash of the first leg. I asked too much which wasn't at all necessary as Gigolo was on very good form. However, maybe it simply made me more alert for the next two tests which turned out to be excellent. I pulled myself together and memories of Atlanta were racing through my mind. That experience helped me to regain my concentration and to fight on. During the freestyle on the final day, Gigolo gave me the greatest feeling. Towards the end of the Kür it felt as if my body was covered in goose pimples! No matter what the outcome would have been, I knew that Gigolo and I had given our best. Nothing else but Gigolo and myself mattered! The joy of knowing that Gigolo had done everything I had asked for was overwhelming!'

So how does Isabell prepare Gigolo for a big occasion? 'It is, again, down to experience. I think that Gigolo has always sensed when it matters most. It is

German trainer Dr Schulten-Baumer and Isabell Werth have been a successful team for over eleven years. Isabell is quick to acknowledge that she would never have reached such heights without the doctor's help. 'Not only is he a superb trainer but he also owns all the horses I ride!'

Isabell Werth waving to a jubilant crowd before receiving the gold medal for her win in the individual contest at the 1997 European Championships. 'I wanted to do well in front of the home crowd.'

that the doctor is right! That he is present at shows gives me tremendous confidence. It is so important to me to have someone I can trust implicitly. The doctor sees things long before they even happen. I can't imagine being able to stay at the top without his help!'

Due to Gigolo's excellence, Isabell doesn't have to prepare him much before entering the arena. 'I ride him for half an hour before the class but would also have taken him out a few hours beforehand just to revise certain movements. I don't believe in spending hours getting a horse ready for a test. You might not believe this but I don't even do much at home with Gigolo. I keep him fit and see that his muscles are well toned. I want him to stay happy. Before big shows I will loosen him up and ride through the choreography of his Kür. If necessary, I will try to refine some movements, specially piaffe and passage. However, I do make sure not to neglect any of his muscles so that he doesn't get sore.'

When winning the 1994 World Championship title Isabell decided to enter the Grand Prix Special as opposed to the Kür. The reason behind that is very precise. 'It has always been very clear to me that true sporting comparison lies in the Grand Prix and the Special because each competitor has to perform the same movement at the same point. As long as the two were divided, the choice was obvious to me. With the Kür you do have the added subjective elements of music and choreography. I think that combining the three was the ideal solution.'

Isabell takes great pleasure in riding the freestyle and believes that it was an inevitable progression for

a feeling of togetherness. No words can explain what actually happens between us. We just understand each other without having to formulate it. It's total harmony.

'Gigolo's strength is that he has no weaknesses! He has three fabulous gaits. I am never afraid of riding any of the compulsory movements. When we slip up it is usually down to me. Most mistakes occur when I surprise him with my aids or when I don't give him enough warning. When it happens, and this might sound very hurtful at the time, the doctor always blames me, never the horse. I admit that the moment the error happens I don't like hearing it but I know

Isabell Werth sharing an emotional moment with millions of spectators around the globe during the playing of the German national anthem in celebration of her Olympic title win in Atlanta. 'At that moment I wasn't aware of how close the public was. It was a very intimate moment where tears of joy, relief and nervous tension were simply running down my cheeks.'

the sport. 'The Kür has brought an additional attraction for the spectators. However, I still maintain that the Special produces tremendous tension. The solution of combining it all is a very fair one. Luck doesn't come into it as much nowadays because one's form is judged over three days. I enjoy the Kür a lot. I try to show off my horse's strength, knowing full well that, at the end of the day, it is just as important to perform all the movements with technical precision.'

Asked what life with horses has meant to her, Isabell's face lit up. 'When alone and working with horses, the necessary concentration, the required discipline and the need to adapt to a living creature are, in themselves, wonderful. It is fascinating to observe how each horse radiates his own personality. All of this is so unique to our sport. I also see dealing with all the people and the sport as the best training for life.'

And to sum up Gigolo, well: 'He is the best friend one would ever want to have. He is always there for me. If I haven't seen him for a few days because I took other horses to a show, I make sure to see him immediately I return. I give him a little treat and then I usually tease him by telling him how well his stable mates did and that he'd better pull his socks up!'

Anky van Grunsven and
Bonfire on their one-time
flying changes routine at the
1997 European Championships,
Verden. Anky was lying first
after the Grand Prix and the
Special but was just pipped
at the line on the final day
by a faultless performance
from Germany's Isabell Werth
and Gigolo. However, Anky
and Bonfire didn't leave
empty handed, winning silver
medals both with the team
and as individuals.

Anky van Grunsven and Bonfire

'Bonfire and I have an incredible bond. Whenever I ride him I have only one thing on *my* mind and that is Bonfire's mind! Our understanding for one another is very deeply rooted. We just both know what each of us is about to do. When we are in the arena I get the feeling that we are one. It's like a bomb could explode and we wouldn't notice it!'

This touching statement comes from Dutch triple Volvo World Cup Champion Anky van Grunsven who has not only won these titles on Bonfire in three consecutive years (1995 to 1997) but has also been crowned National Champion with Bonfire seven years in a row from 1991 to 1997. The pair's success also includes a team silver medal at the 1992 Barcelona Olympics as well as a team and individual silver medal at the 1996 Atlanta Olympics.

Anky, whose parents own a construction company, was born into a horse-loving family. Anky and her two older brothers started off on ponies before moving on to horses. 'I had a Shetland pony that I brushed for a whole year before I finally decided to sit on it!' Anky

started riding horses at the age of twelve when she was given a hand-me-down horse by one of her brothers. Soon after that her father bought her Prisco, a horse she brought on to Grand Prix level and on which she gained her ticket to the 1988 Seoul Olympics. Looking for an additional horse, Anky and her father came across Bonfire and bought him as a two and a half year old from a Dutch dealer.

Anky began to compete with Bonfire when he was five and managed to move him through to Grand Prix level when he was only seven. 'Bonfire showed such talent and learned all the difficult movements with such ease that I never had the feeling that he wouldn't cope. The only difficulty I encountered was his exuberance. He is such a high spirited horse and he was very hot and I had a problem to settle him down. Riding him in Grand Prix tests gave him more to think about. Prix St Georges and Intermediaire I were far too simple for him.'

However, Anky and Bonfire really only came of age when she decided to ask her boyfriend, the

Dutch trainer Sjef Janssen is the man behind Anky's success. He used to compete himself but, of late, is concentrating on schooling horses and training riders from around the world. British rider Jane Bredin and Cupido are also regular visitors to his yard.

Anky van Grunsven and nine-year-old German-bred Bonfire performing in extended canter during the 1992 Barcelona Olympics. Riding at her second Olympics, Anky helped the Dutch team to win a silver medal and was placed fourth overall in the individual competition. 'My goal was to be placed among the top ten but I never anticipated getting as close as I did. We were fifth in the Grand Prix and fourth overall. A great team spirit and very good training made all the difference!'

international rider Sjef Janssen, to help her. 'I had had a few different trainers but at one point I thought that Bonfire could do much more than I was able to get out of him. I felt stuck but knew that we were both capable of more. I just didn't know how.'

Sjef and Anky started to train together and haven't looked back since. 'Sjef is always searching for more and yet he makes it all simpler. It's not that other trainers made it seem difficult but I find our way of training more logical. Sjef looks deeper and if something doesn't work one way he figures out another way! He has a completely different approach to training from anybody else I know. His method is

more inventive but it also pushes the horse harder. Sometimes we try things that don't work but at least we will have tried and have realised that it doesn't work. Sjef believes that getting into trouble is very good because it prompts horse and rider to think and to find a way out of the problem. That approach really helped me. Normally, you don't want to make mistakes during training but Sjef believes that it is helpful to make mistakes when you're training because if you never make mistakes you never learn. If you only do things well, you will never improve and never reach your true potential.'

Anky loves to teach too and believes it to be very

Anky van Grunsven and Bonfire during the piaffe at the 1997 European Championships, one of the movements Bonfire is most famous for. 'Sure I was disappointed to lose the lead on the final day but, then again, I never thought that I would win the European in Verden. I was, however, extremely pleased with Bonfire's performance over the three days. He showed real consistency!'

educational. She runs her own business and usually rides up to eight horses a day.

Now aged fourteen, Bonfire has settled down considerably but Anky remembers how difficult he once was. 'Bonfire has a lot of Thoroughbred in him which might explain why he was so overactive and excited at first. He never had a problem with learning the movements. It was just finding a way of settling him down which took time. Even a couple of years ago he could still be afraid of entering the arena. Once he was in the arena he familiarised himself with it and felt safe.

'Bonfire is rather special. I do connect with other horses too but with Bonfire it's really unique. The understanding we share is very difficult to describe. Usually I am a down to earth person and don't believe in inexplicable things, however, there is no doubt in my mind that Bonfire and I are experiencing something out of the ordinary.'

Anky admits that she didn't feel this closeness right from the beginning but because Bonfire was so difficult and because she knew how talented he was, she felt it important to concentrate on him. 'If I didn't pay attention or didn't concentrate for only one split second, it meant that something was about to happen. Perhaps we are so close because I gave Bonfire all my attention and learned to know him. When I sit on him, there is no time to think about anything else but him because he is so alert. He is so very intelligent! I believe that at this level horses have to be extremely intelligent.'

Anky simply glows when she is chatting about Bonfire but her second favourite topic is definitely talking about the Kür. 'I love to ride to music! It gives me such a good feeling and makes me very happy. The music I choose for my Kür is very important to me. I need to love the music I ride to. It gives me a feeling of being able to fly to the music! Everything seems that much easier when I ride to music. It's the rhythm.

Anky van Grunsven and Gere (NL), CDIO, Aachen 1995.

It's like dancing. Riding a Kür is more challenging. You have to ride your horse, you have to watch the music and you have to watch your test. No matter how difficult it is, it always puts me in a good mood! The reason why I chose to ride the Kür in The Hague was because I believe that the Kür saved our sport.'

Winning the Kür and becoming World Champion in her own country at the 1994 World Equestrian Games in The Hague meant a great deal to Anky.

'Before The Hague I always rode the Special because the better horse and rider combinations always competed in the Special. My father felt that I should do the same in The Hague but I said to him that we should change that trend. I insisted that this time the Grand Prix was more important than the Special and that I would have to prove myself in the Grand Prix instead because all the competitors were in it. As it happened, Bonfire and I won the Grand Prix and, by winning the Kür too, I didn't get the feeling of not having achieved much. In fact, it was very exciting for me. It was great to see and feel the crowd's reaction to my Kür. I made a slight mistake in one of my pirouettes so it was always going to be close. When I had won, everybody went crazy. People tried to climb the fence at the stable area. They were screaming, singing and yelling. It is a wonderful feeling when you ride a nice test and people get pleasure out of it. But it is almost unbelievable when people are as euphoric as they were then.'

Asked whether she gets bored riding Grand Prix or Special tests at most shows, Anky was quick to reply

Anky van Grunsven showing off the gold medal she won for her Kür performance at the 1994 World Equestrian Games in The Hague. Anky had to convince her father that choosing the Kür as opposed to the Special was going to set a trend that would make winning the Kür just as important as winning the Special. After seeing Anky and Bonfire run through their Kür in training, Mr van Grunsven had no reservations at all!

that she never gets bored but that the horses might. 'I am fortunate enough to have a few top class horses. Riding the same test is therefore so very different with every horse. Riders have the chance to do the best they can every time. This is a big incentive.'

Riding to perfection and noticing that everything is falling into place gives riders a feeling of elation. It is no different for Anky. 'When you look at the video of my Kür at the 1997 World Cup Final in Hertogenbosch you can see that towards the end of the test I have this big smile on my face! All I am thinking is: "This is so much fun!" The first couple of minutes into the test I usually try to figure out how the horse is reacting to the situation and how he feels. When I sense that all is well, I feel as if nothing could go wrong. Of course I don't always get that feeling and I have to keep my concentration. However, this complete feeling happens perhaps once a year.'

Most recently, Anky remembers feeling totally delighted with her and Bonfire's performance during the Grand Prix at the 1997 European Championships in Verden. However, good though their performance was over the three days, the pair were beaten into second place by German Champion Isabell Werth. 'I wasn't really disappointed not to get the gold medal because I knew before travelling to Verden that I wouldn't win it. That doesn't mean to say that I don't think that Bonfire should have won. I believe he deserved to win because he only made one little mistake over the three days. None of the other horses had been as consistent as Bonfire. So I am more disappointed for Bonfire, for his record. Bonfire exudes

so much happiness when he performs. His ears are always pricked and it is for all to see how hard he tries and how much he enjoys himself. Okay, his walk might not be the best in the world but his piaffe and passage are out of this world!'

Anky's sense of fun really comes alive when she rides for pleasure and during exhibition displays. 'I really enjoy riding at exhibitions. You can try different things, be more creative and risk a little more. I am also more relaxed. It's more fun for the spectators too. You can play around with the lighting. When you are competing it is so important that you get everything right. There is hardly room for any mistakes. I do get more of a rush of adrenaline when I compete because the desire to win heightens my nervous tension. Competing is therefore more exciting. I like to be the best!

'In a strange sort of way I was the happiest person in Verden because I thought that I had done such a good job over the three days. The most important thing for me was that I rode really well. I made one mistake in the two-time flying changes. That's all. Apart from that I was so concentrated and I felt I rode my tests as well as I ride them at home. It is important for me to keep my nerves under control, not to make silly mistakes and not to be a second behind what I have to do.'

Talking about the 1996 Atlanta Olympics raised quite different emotions. 'I don't want to talk about Atlanta! It was the most awful week in my entire life! The day before the Grand Prix the hotel management made us get out of bed at midnight because of a bomb

scare. So we sat on the street for two hours! However, I was really pleased with my Grand Prix test. I was also pleased with the Special. Then my grandmother died so I was upset on the one hand but also very happy about being in the lead. I had such mixed emotions! Then came the drama of the vet check when Bonfire didn't pass the vet at first. It was the worst nightmare, knowing that I was in the lead but having to wait five hours before the jury finally passed him. Once we were cleared I only had fifteen minutes of training session left. I quickly threw a saddle on him. Needless to say, the training went down the drain. From that moment on I knew that all was lost. On the morning of the final the training wasn't too bad but during the freestyle I felt that my spirit had left me. Reflecting on it I can say that I lost the gold medal

Anky van Grunsven and Bonfire flat out on their lap of honour after the prizegiving ceremony at the 1996 Atlanta Olympics. Anky is always ready to show her emotions and thank a supporting crowd.

before I even entered the arena to ride the Kür.

'Wining an Olympic gold medal is important to me. However, I think that to win gold one has to have a very lucky week and I had a terrible week. So for a bad week I guess I did really well!'

No matter how stressful life at the top of her chosen sport can be, Anky is a very resolute person with a healthy philosophy of life. 'I have a really good life. I am a happy person. Yes, I have my downs like everybody else. Like in Atlanta. I really had had it after that week! But I told myself to forget about it and I just focused on all my young horses at home. I have put the experience behind me. It's gone! One can think about how unlucky one has been for a long time but so what! Yes, I have been unlucky but life goes on! I don't see any other way of dealing with life. One could be sad a whole year but it's not worth it. There is more to life than being sad!'

Anky van Grunsven during the prizegiving of the individual honours at the 1996 Atlanta Olympics. 'I was so very happy. My smile says it all. Okay, I was disappointed for three minutes about not having won the individual gold medal but then I was so excited about having won two silver medals. We had a big party that night!'

German riders Nicole Uphoff-
Becker and Isabell Werth
were finally able to release
the nervous tension that
surrounded the champion-
ships and give each other
a hug during the prizegiving
ceremony of the 1992
Barcelona Olympics. Nicole
had successfully regained her
Olympic title and Isabell had
secured the individual silver
medal. Together they were
members of the gold-winning
German team. Nicole recalls
winning being a huge relief.
Isabell had to deal with a lot
of pressure because the press
had made her the favourite
following her win at the
European Championships
the year before. Isabell
went one better four years
later in Atlanta by winning
both the team and the
individual gold medal. Both
ladies maintain that they
have a lot of respect for
one another's achievements.

WINNING MOMENTS

Winning – time to celebrate! Time to finally let go of all the tension and utmost concentration that competitors experience throughout a championship! It's all over! It's time for competitors to savour the fruits of their hard work – well, only until the next important show or championship that is! The international dressage calendar suggests that top competitors travel almost every week from event to event in search of victory and then once a year to a major championship where either a European or a World title is on offer, not to mention the Olympics every four years. It is before and during those significant occasions that riders feel the gradual build up of anticipation, apprehension, perhaps even stress, and most certainly pressure. The better form a partnership displays in the run up to a championship, the higher the expectations of winning. So it's hardly surprising that the favourites among the competitors show signs of strain during an event. The media can also sometimes hype up situations before and during a competition, by making a particular partnership clear favourites, or by inventing unfriendly rivalry between top title contenders, all of which must inevitably add to the riders' stress. Suspense looms over the participants throughout a championship. Competitors are eager to give their best, keen to perform as close to perfection as possible and desperate to give their

horses the best possible chance to do their best.

What better reward can you imagine than being placed first or being hailed a champion! Winning is what feeds the hungry competitor's soul.

Some dressage riders are delighted when they have finished their dressage test. Some thank their horse for a superb ride. Others wave to their fans in recognition of the received support. Very rarely will a dressage rider give more than a wave though. In many ways this is understandable because dressage is about precision, control, calmness and composure. The audience sense an air of serenity when watching horse and rider in action. Once the test is over, however, the spectators are very keen to applaud to show their support of the competitors. From a spectator's point of view it is very satisfying to share the rider's delight. And how nice it is to see a rider smile or wave back to the crowd!

In dressage, the competitors never know how their performance has been received by the judges until the marks pop up on the scoreboard.

Some riders might sense that their performance has been sufficient to win them the class or the championship but they can never be completely sure nor can they relax until the final score is made official. Dressage is not as straightforward as show jumping or three day eventing. There, the rider

Champagne celebration – Hermès dressage day, Royal Windsor 1997.

knows immediately he or she crosses the finishing line what their score has been. In championships, competitors enter the arena in reverse order of their placing, which means that the riders who have been best placed will go last. This adds to the excitement.

that reveal a sentiment. I remember following Isabell Werth through my lens during the entire duration of her Kür at the 1997 European Championships in Verden, Germany. The pressure was fully on Isabell who was lying 0.38 per cent behind Anky van

Individual medallists from the 1994 World Equestrian Games, Nicole Uphoff-Becker (silver), Isabell Werth (gold) and Sven Rothenberger (bronze) all seemed delighted with their placings. Isabell and Nicole were also members of the gold-medal-winning German team. Sven was particularly pleased with his achievements. The Hague was the first show he had competed at for his newly adopted country, The Netherlands. His performances on Dondolo, a horse he had started to ride only five weeks prior to the games, were also rewarded with a team silver medal.

'The show was fabulous! Winning the bronze was really an unexpected result. I was especially proud because I had only ridden Dondolo for thirty-five days before arriving in The Hague!'

In dressage, however, the suspense of knowing who has won gets slightly prolonged.

As a photographer, I seek images that mark a winning occasion, such as pictures showing a rider's delight, which will give us a real taste of the passion they feel for their sport. Although it is very satisfying to capture a horse and rider executing a movement to perfection, the most rewarding shots are still the ones

Grunsven and Bonfire before the freestyle. She was as concentrated and poker faced as only she can be. Gigolo was giving his best. Isabell's aids were as invisible as always. Suddenly, towards the end of their test, as Gigolo was performing a circle in passage, I noticed that Isabell's face muscles had started to relax. A fraction later, as they came out of the circle, Isabell showed the trace of a smile! It was beautiful to see! Isabell's self-confidence undoubtedly had grown throughout the Kür. She must have felt that the fluency and harmony she was experiencing with Gigolo would win her the European title, which indeed they did!

It is during the actual prizegiving ceremonies, however, that winners show their utter delight most freely. It is not unusual for newly crowned Olympic champions to shed floods of tears while their country's flag rises to the music of their national anthem. Nicole Uphoff-Becker couldn't hold back her emotions at the 1992 Barcelona Olympics where she defended both of her titles, as individual and team champion, from four years previously. Isabell Werth surrendered to the same emotion while the German anthem was played following her win in Atlanta.

When whole teams are rewarded, the atmosphere is generally much more relaxed. The team members support each other while standing on the rostrum and big smiles are substituted for tears!

Some of the joyous moments that riders experience are reflected in the following pages.

A very happy Anky van Grunsven after finishing her Grand Prix on Bonfire at the 1996 Atlanta Olympics. The pair won the test and stayed in front of Isabell Werth up until the freestyle, when Isabell managed to turn the tables. Sadly, Anky had to handle the emotional upset of losing her grandmother on the day of the Special, so winning the team as well as the individual silver medal was a tremendous accomplishment!

'I was so happy with Bonfire's form on the day. The crowds were superb and it's always nice to be able to acknowledge them at the end of the test.'

A delighted Monica Theodorescu on her lap of honour with the Hanoverian gelding Grunox after winning the Grand Prix at the CDIO in Aachen. Although all of the dressage competitions take place in the smaller surroundings of the dressage stadium, the prizegiving for the international dressage events is held in the main show jumping arena in front of a huge crowd.

'The nice thing about the crowds in Aachen is that they are so enthusiastic! Spectators around the dressage arena are very knowledgeable which creates an electrifying atmosphere. For most people, coming to Aachen is a real tradition. I myself have competed there without fail since the age of nineteen. Being applauded by an even bigger crowd during the prizegiving is a unique feeling!'

In the eighties, British three day event rider Christopher Bartle took a few years out of his number one sport to concentrate on dressage when the Irish-bred Wily Trout, aged nine, sustained a slight tendon injury which kept him out of eventing. Because Wily Trout showed talent in dressage, Chris decided to take up the new challenge of bringing him on to Grand Prix level. Initially, Chris never thought that they would go as far as representing Great Britain internationally. However, between 1981 and 1986 the pair did just that. Their most notable achievements were sixth place individually at the 1984 Los Angeles Olympics, fourth place at the 1985 European Championships held in Copenhagen and second place at the inaugural World Cup Final in 1986. This picture was taken at the 1987 European Championships at Goodwood, after which eighteen-year-old Wily Trout, still full of going, was officially retired. Chris believes that Wily Trout really made a name for himself in the freestyle.

'With Wily Trout being Irish, I chose an Irish song called 'The Irish Washer Woman' for his piaffe, passage routine. Thanks to us it became quite a well-known piece of music! Wily Trout was such a positive horse which made up for his physical weakness and lack of natural aptitude for dressage. Basically, he didn't know what the meaning of slowing down was! His workaholic attitude was a great asset to him. He was still as enthusiastic and full of energy as ever on the day of his retirement. He didn't have extravagant paces but he had attitude. He always wanted to work and please. He was the most positive horse you could ever ask for! If he was a person he would have been Linford Christie!'

All smiles in the British Team after coming second in the 1996 CDIO at Aachen. If it wasn't for the home team, the Brits, consisting of Ferdi Eilberg, Richard Davison, Vicky Thompson and Dr Wilfried Bechtolsheimer, would have won!

FERDI EILBERG: 'Coming second that year was a tremendous feeling. We hadn't quite expected coming so close. It was a special occasion and we all drew an extra bit of encouragement from it. I remember our horses getting quite excited during the prizegiving which takes place in the main stadium. Richard's horse Askari took off coming past the main stand and ran towards the winning team. Once Richard had regained control he told us that it had been the first time he had been part of the German team!'

RICHARD DAVISON: 'Aachen is like the Wimbledon of dressage! It has an amazing atmosphere which I always notice when sitting in the competitors' stands. It's quiet and yet electric. Aachen holds a special place in every dressage rider's career. Askari was only nine in 1996. Coming second with the team was a very good boost before leaving for Atlanta. The prizegiving in Aachen is absolutely amazing. This is when you suddenly notice a change in the atmosphere. As you ride through the tunnel the noise of the crowd certainly hits you! Askari is a remarkable horse. If he was human he'd be a schoolboy, not only a prefect but probably also house captain. His report would read: "Always tries hard, good manners and neat work." Secretly, however, I wouldn't put it past him to nip behind the bicycle shed for a quick cigarette!'

VICKY THOMPSON: 'Coming second with the team was great fun. I think that when you are riding for the team every rider tries to ride to their maximum. Not that the strategy changes too much because you need the marks so I don't take real risks but you still have to know your horse well enough to get the best possible score. Enfant was quite sharp in Aachen. However, he got a score of almost 68 per cent, his highest marks ever. Enfant is a horse full of enthusiasm, bursting with life. He fitted me like a well-worn glove!'

DR BECHTOLSHEIMER: 'This was my first time in Aachen and coming second was a great experience. It is a memory I will treasure! Giorgione also knew it was Aachen. I felt that he was really trying. I remember being halfway through the test and thinking how well he was going. I thought we only had to try a little harder to really crack it but then I overdid it a fraction which led to messing up the second pirouette. However, I always enjoy riding under a bit of pressure in a competitive environment.'

(Left) Apart from winning a team bronze medal at the 1994 World Equestrian Games, Carol Lavell took home bad memories from The Hague! 'My score was actually the drop score. Gifted injured himself in Brussels where we were stabled before travelling to the games. He did a somersault and fell on the pavement which meant that he wasn't in such good form in The Hague as I would have wanted him to be. However, our marks were solid enough to get us into the freestyle. Robert Dover, Kathleen Raine and Gary Rockwell did a great job and the only good thing I remember is that the US got another team medal!'

(Right) Klaus Balkenhol, Isabell Werth, Monica Theodorescu and Martin Schaudt sharing a joke after receiving the team gold medals for their efforts at the Atlanta Olympics.
KLAUS BALKENHOL: I believe that we all started to laugh uncontrollably because I told the two ladies to be a bit more serious! Winning this time round was fantastic. However, our victory in Barcelona was even more overwhelming, especially as Goldstern had also topped his performance by winning an individual bronze medal there. To accomplish something one has always admired in others is a tremendous feeling!'
ISABELL WERTH: 'Winning with the team is fabulous, especially because over the past three years the Dutch have really challenged us. This means that all members have to produce a great test. This might increase the pressure for each of us within the team but, at the same time, it makes winning more special!'
MONICA THEODORESCU: 'Although it is my third Olympic gold medal with the team, it is never an easy task. It is already difficult enough to make the team, let alone win! We all showed a lot of enthusiasm in Atlanta and then to have won was just brilliant. Only those who have won a gold medal can appreciate how difficult it actually is!'
MARTIN SCHAUDT: 'I think we all showed a lot of nervous tension during the competition. Winning was just a huge relief! I can't really remember what was said that made us laugh. I believe it was just a complete letting go of the stress we had been put under. Once the weight has been lifted one can laugh at practically anything!'

Jane Bredin, Jennie Loriston-Clarke, Joanna Jackson and Ferdi Eilberg made up the team taking third place at the 1995 CDIO in Aachen. Making sure that things ran smoothly for the team was Jane Bartle-Wilson acting as chef d'équipe.

JANE BREDIN: This was my first appearance in Aachen and it felt just like a dream come true. Cupido was tenth in both the Grand Prix and the Special which meant that I was in the line up twice! Riding in Aachen was a fantastic experience. I remember that Susie, Cupido's owner, and I just walked around in a state of shock most of the time! I believe that it's the most special show for a dressage rider because no one goes there if they don't think they are capable of doing a reasonably good job. I remember Jennie being so supportive and coming up to me showing true enthusiasm about my placings!'

JENNIE LORISTON-CLARKE: 'The first time I travelled to Aachen must have been in the sixties when I rode Desert Storm! I remember having been rather gobsmacked as you might say! It is almost a bigger thing to do well in Aachen than at the Olympics but it takes place every year! Aachen is really the mecca. Dressage riders are also rubbing shoulders with the show jumpers which gives it a fantastic atmosphere. Being on the British team is always a great honour. In 1995 we had a really fabulous team with a great team spirit.'

JOANNA JACKSON: 'Nothing compares to riding in Aachen! It was a fantastic experience and I was happy that the team did so well. Mester Mouse is fabulous to ride and seems always to rise to the occasion. He is a lovely horse to have. He simply loves showing off to the crowd. I started riding him when he was eight. He was virtually unbeaten in England when we were competing in Young Riders. He is eighteen now and 1998 will be his last season. He has got to be at the centre of attention at all times!

'Mester Mouse used to be quite a nightmare actually! I remember taking him to his first show. We were trotting up to the judges' box when he suddenly stopped dead and bolted off in the opposite direction refusing to go anywhere near the judges! He was quite exuberant, sharp and spooky but it soon all turned into more of a sparkle. He is my dream horse and he will always be special to me!'

FERDI EILBERG: 'Aachen is a special show for me because I first went to Aachen in 1970 as a groom for Dr Reiner Klimke. From 1974 to 1976 I was there as a trainer. In 1986, when Aachen held the Show Jumping World Championships, I won the freestyle with Giovani. Now I have competed there a few times with Arun Thor and he has always been a good boy! Riding in the team usually adds to the excitement. I hold good memories of 1995, specially of having Jennie on the team because she is always such a great back up!'

Ignacio Rambla, Director of the Royal Andalusian School of Equestrian Art, warmed the crowd's hearts by performing the Spanish walk with the twelve-year-old Andalusian stallion Evento during the prizegiving at the 1997 European Championships in Verden. Ignacio was born and bred in Jerez de la Frontera, home of the Real Escuela Andaluza del Arte Ecuestre. He joined the school as an apprentice in 1978 and started touring the world with the school. In 1983 he moved up a rank and became an instructor within the school. Ten years on, Ignacio also began to compete at international level. Together with Evento, Ignacio has retained the title of National Dressage Champion since 1995. At the Atlanta Olympics, as well as in Verden, the pair were placed eleventh individually. Evento is owned by the military stud of Jerez where he covers mares regularly. He is the most popular horse when performing at the school's shows, whether in Spain or at any other spectacle around the world. He has fans everywhere he goes. During the Atlanta Olympics, Evento received hundreds of cards from his American admirers.

The Dutch all-girl team of Ellen Bontje, Annemarie Sanders, Tineke Bartels and Anky van Grunsven took the team silver medal behind the Germans but ahead of the Americans at the 1992 Barcelona Olympics.

TINEKE BARTELS: 'Winning the silver medal was very exciting for us because it was the first Olympic medal in dressage for Holland. Needless to say, we were overjoyed! I can say this in retrospect because we won the silver medal again in Atlanta and although we were also very happy there, we were not as thrilled as in Barcelona! The first time is always special! I had difficulties making the team but, once I had made it, I was happy that my nerves didn't let me down. I was cool and Courage gave his best ever test which was fantastic!'

ELLEN BONTJE: 'Winning the silver medal with the team was one of my greatest sporting achievements! We knew that we had a good chance of a medal but we didn't know how strong the Americans were going to be. When we won the silver, we simply went wild!'

ANKY VAN GRUNSVEN: 'We had a lot of fun in Barcelona. When driving home after the prizegiving we each had our medals around our neck. Cruising along on our way back into town we wound the windows down and were screaming and singing, waving our medals at the poor passersby who didn't know what we were up to!'

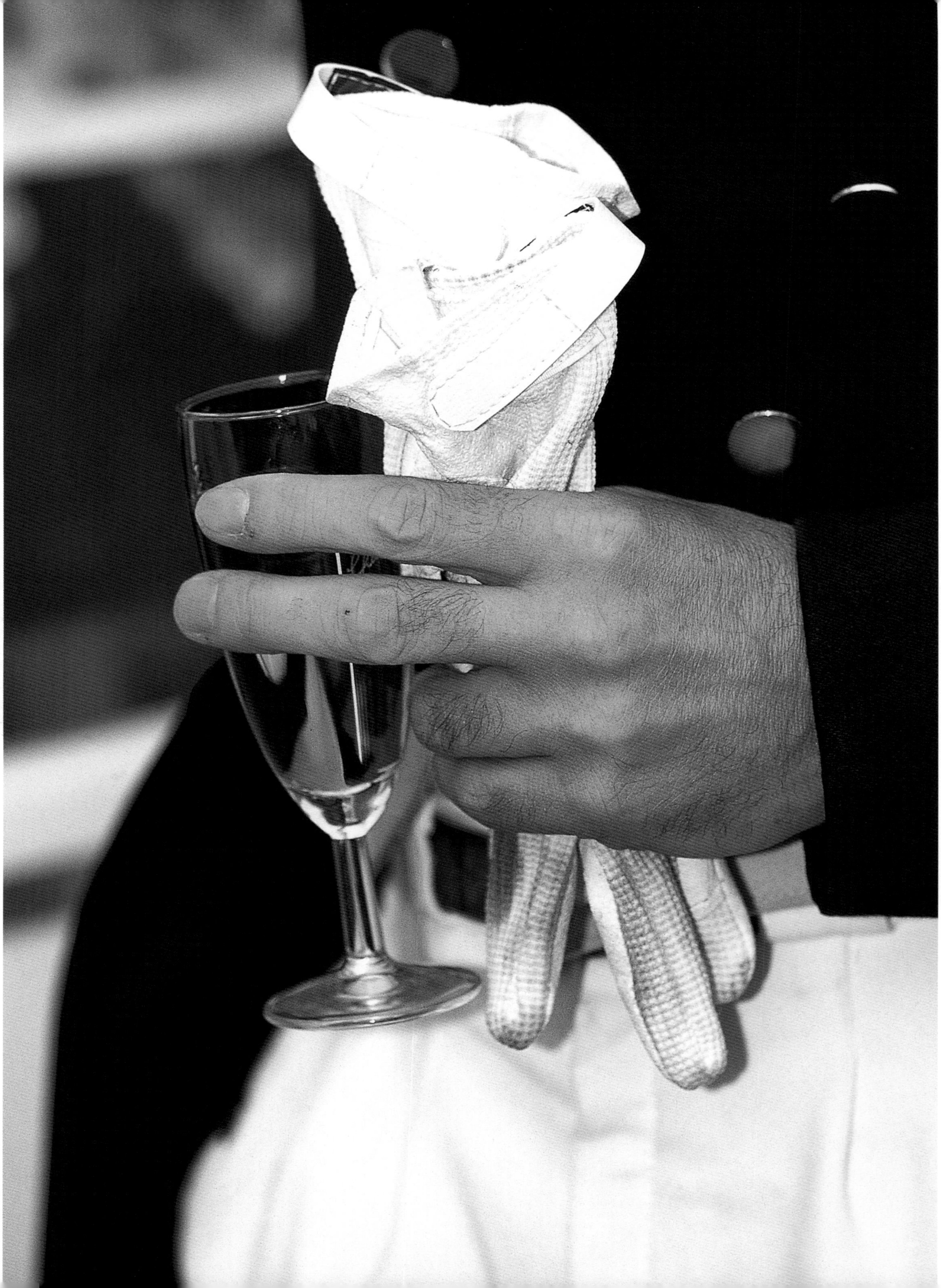

LASTING
IMPRESSIONS

(Clockwise from far left)
Dr W. Bechtoldsheimer (GB),
CDIO, Aachen 1996; Russian
rider, Verden 1997; German
dressage rider, CDIO, Aachen
1995; Christine Stückelberger
(Sui), Atlanta Olympics 1996.

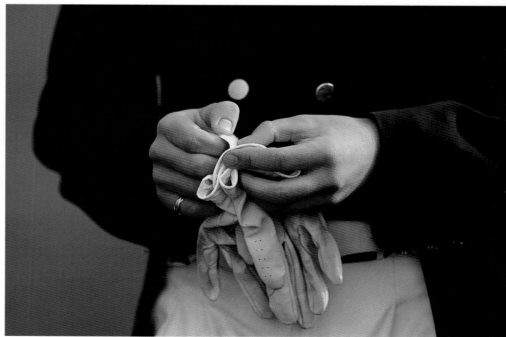

(Clockwise from top left)
German dressage rider, CDIO,
Aachen 1995; Carl Hester
(GB), Addington 1995; Peter
Storr (GB), National
Championships, Addington
1995; Martin Schaudt (Ger),
Atlanta Olympics 1996.

Peter Storr (GB), Addington 1995.

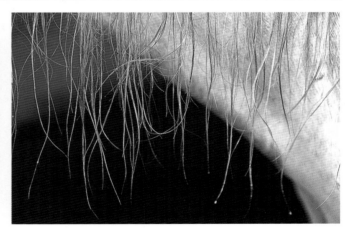

(Far left) Arnaldo Thor, Dominique D'Esmé's horse after their test, CDIO, Hickstead 1997.

(Above and left) Lusitano horses, Portugal, June 1997.

(Clockwise from top left)
Margit Otto-Crépin (Fr),
Atlanta Olympics 1996;
Desirée Puccini (Ita), CDIO,
Aachen 1995; Margit Otto-
Crépin (Fr), Atlanta Olympics
1996; Caroline Hatlapa (Aut),
Verden 1997.

Cadre Noir rider
M. Souveton.

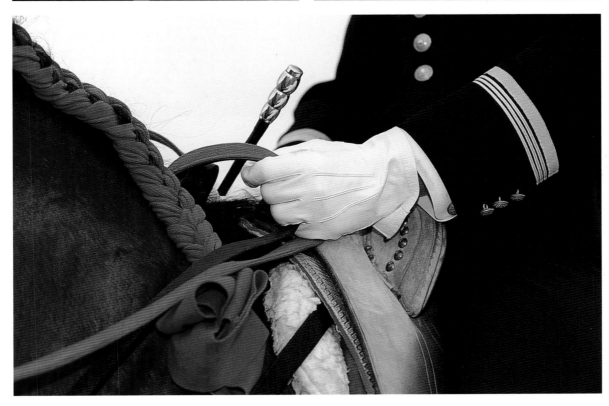

(Above left) Georg Wahl,
trainer of Christine
Stückelberger, Verden 1997.

(Above right) Peter Storr's
groom, CDIO, Hickstead 1997.

Eric Lette, Chairman of the
FEI Dressage Committee,
acknowledging a rider's salute.

INDEX

ANNIE MACDONALD-HALL   ULLA SALZGEBER   EMILE FAURIE   FRANCISCO BESSA DE CARVALHO   JANE BREDIN

SUSIE CUMINE   ARTHUR KOTTAS-HELDENBERG   CAROL LAVELL   RICHARD DAVISON   ALVARO DOMECQ

ANKY VAN GRUNSVEN   NADINE CAPELLMANN-BIFFAR   FERDI EILBERG   CHRISTOPHER BARTLE   JEAN LOUIS GUNTZ

ANNA MERVELDT   DR WILFRIED BECHTOLSHEIMER   ANDREAS HARRER   JENNIE LORISTON-CLARKE

VICKY THOMPSON   ELLEN BONTJE   IGNACIO RAMBLA ALGARIN   ISABELL WERTH   JOANNA JACKSON